Advance praise for Writing

This is a must-read for school leaders and teachers. Based on both research and the "wisdom of practice," it offers a wealth of teaching strategies to boost the achievement and happiness of boys in school. A new contribution is how to use the web to find boy-friendly activities. If you can only read one book about how to reach boys, this is it.

Judith Kleinfeld, Director of the Boys Project,
Professor of Psychology Emeritus,
University of Alaska

Writing the Playbook *is an incredible resource that students love, teachers appreciate, and administrators are learning from. It provides the solutions that school systems globally are desperately searching for regarding the behavior and academic performance of boys. It is written in a way that is engaging, empowering, and inspiring to those in all levels of education. If you've ever desired a positive educational atmosphere, this book provides the blueprint!*

Chris Cannon, Author of *Winning Back Our Boys:
The Ultimate Game Plan for Teachers and Parents*

Boys and girls can differ vastly in how they most effectively learn. As educational leaders it is critical that we create school environments that clearly reflect and demonstrate this understanding. This insightful book will inform, guide, and transform the way you lead in schools. This is a great resource that will definitely produce results!

Don Haddad, EdD, Superintendent of Schools,
St. Vrain Valley School District

As I read this book I am thrilled Kelley King is speaking out on behalf of our boys! While they sit motionless in the traditional classrooms and feel abandoned by education, she makes the case for justified changes. We owe it to them to acknowledge the differences and to design an educational experience that honors them. No longer can we, as citizens of this country, allow those so-called experts to claim that boys and girls are the same and ask our schools to ignore the obvious differences. Enough! Bring on the strategies for our boys that will allow teachers to inspire them to greatness!

Kim Bevill, Director of Gray Matters &
Educational Consultant

This book should be required reading for every teaching credential candidate and educator. Its neurobiological approach to learning and behavior is not rocket science; it's long overdue common sense. Bravo!

Joe Manthey, Education Consultant
and Seminar Leader

As a lifelong feminist and the grandmother of three boys just starting school, I am passionately interested in boys being taken "as they are" and taught in ways that will help them develop. For a long time we worried about girls, who are presently thriving in school and beyond. It's boys' turn now! Yes, men still "rule" out in the world, but in school many boys are falling behind. For a strong America, we need both genders to thrive and to lead. And King's book will help us get to that America.

Dottie Lamm, MSW, *Denver Post* Columnist,
Former First Lady of Colorado

This is a must-read for school leaders. King, an expert on bridging the gender gap in schools, asks them to try to see things through "the boy lens," which is absolutely necessary today when so many boys aren't coming close to reaching their full educational potential. She offers practical advice for making schools boy friendly, which works just fine for girls too. I applaud her passion, dedication, and expertise. Here's a book that can truly make a positive difference for our society and its future.

Mark Sherman, PhD, Emeritus Professor of Psychology at SUNY,
New Paltz, Editor of Boys and Young Men:
Attention Must Be Paid, a blog sponsored by the Boys Initiative

In my heart I believe that our husbands, sons, and brothers can write and read as well as their female relatives. They all have the ideas and the brilliance. Kelley's book is a guide to support all educators in making those ideas become reality. If we collaborate as educators and as parents, we can make sure that both boys and girls are challenged and supported in schools so that their dreams all become reality.

Dr. Cynthia Stevenson, Superintendent,
Jeffco Public Schools

There is widespread consensus that our young males are not achieving to their full potential. We know the problems. It is time we tackle them, and it is time we foster leadership among those in positions of authority who can make change happen. Kelley's book is an important step in this direction—by calling on school leaders to become engaged and by giving them the tools to make change happen.

Dennis Barbour, Co-Founder and
CEO, Boys Initiative

WRITING THE PLAYBOOK

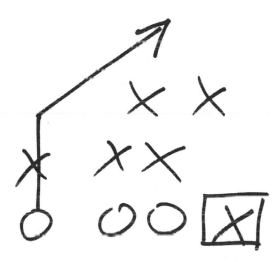

For my son, Connor, a true boy if there ever was one: You have challenged me to see education differently, and you have fueled my desire to help teachers teach boys like you.

For my daughter, Roxy, who makes her teachers' jobs easy: May your generation be filled with men who are as self-directed and high-achieving as you.

For my husband, Chris, who teaches our children every day, through his actions and words, what it means to be a man of integrity: What a difference it would make in this world if every child had a father like you.

WRITING THE PLAYBOOK

A Practitioner's Guide to
Creating a Boy-Friendly School

Foreword by
Michael Gurian,
Author of *The Minds of Boys* and *Boys and Girls Learn Differently!*

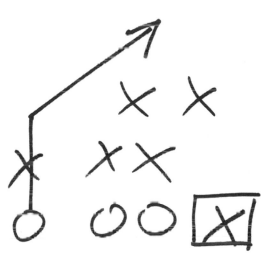

Kelley King

CORWIN
A SAGE Company

CORWIN
A SAGE Company

FOR INFORMATION:

Corwin

A SAGE Company

2455 Teller Road

Thousand Oaks, California 91320

(800) 233-9936

www.corwin.com

SAGE Publications Ltd.

1 Oliver's Yard

55 City Road

London EC1Y 1SP

United Kingdom

SAGE Publications India Pvt. Ltd.

B 1/I 1 Mohan Cooperative Industrial Area

Mathura Road, New Delhi 110 044

India

SAGE Publications Asia-Pacific Pte. Ltd.

3 Church Street

#10-04 Samsung Hub

Singapore 049483

Acquisitions Editor: Arnis Burvikovs

Associate Editor: Desirée A. Bartlett

Editorial Assistant: Mayan N. White

Production Editor: Cassandra Margaret Seibel

Copy Editor: Terri Lee Paulsen

Typesetter: C&M Digitals (P) Ltd.

Proofreader: Caryne Brown

Indexer: Jean Casalegno

Cover Designer: Bryan Fishman

Permissions Editor: Jennifer Barron

Printed in the United States of America.

A catalog record of this book is available from the Library of Congress.

ISBN 978-1-4522-4298-9

This book is printed on acid-free paper.

SUSTAINABLE FORESTRY INITIATIVE

Certified Chain of Custody
Promoting Sustainable Forestry
www.sfiprogram.org
SFI-01268

SFI label applies to text stock

13 14 15 16 17 10 9 8 7 6 5 4 3 2 1

Contents

Additional materials and resources related to
*Writing the Playbook: A Practitioner's Guide to
Creating a Boy-Friendly School* can be found at
www.boyfriendlyschools.com. Kelley King can
be reached at kelleykingpd@hotmail.com.

Foreword

Educators are under immense pressure in this new millennium. Some of those educators, like Kelley King, become visionaries for the sake of students and school systems. Kelley's vision emerged in our national consciousness in 2005, and I am so glad it did. Because Kelley has pursued both the intellectual rigor and the practical delivery of the strategies in this *Playbook*, many schools and students are doing better, achieving more, and enjoying the learning experience in which they spend so much of their day.

I first met Kelley in 2005 by phone. She called to tell me that she and her staff had closed a troubling literacy gap in one year by integrating the theory and practice in *Boys and Girls Learn Differently!* into her school's classroom improvement initiative. She was principal at that time of Douglass Elementary School in the Boulder Valley School District in Boulder, Colorado. To close a boys' literacy gap in one year is no small feat, and Kelley and her staff were celebrating the success. I was honored to help her publicize the success through contacts at *Newsweek* and the TV media, and by inviting her to join our Gurian Institute team, which she did the next year.

As she is doing in the book you are about to read, Kelley teaches educational success at the achievement data level, but also at many other levels. First, her school was an example of what happens when all teachers in a system are attuned to the learning needs of girls and boys; once staff gained understanding and training related to gender differences in learning, they (and, thus, the whole school climate as an aggregate) systematically changed to improve teacher effectiveness and student performance. Douglass Elementary had done that in 2004–2005, and in the last six years, Kelley has helped many other schools do that, as you will read in these pages.

Second, her school was an example of the power of teaching teachers about both the nurture and *nature* of gender differences in learning. Most of us hear a lot about nurture as a source of things in our teacher training, and very little about nature. That mistake can haunt us as we operate in classrooms in which we sense how differently many of the boys and girls are learning, and feel unable to help all of our students learn. The approach Kelley and her team used to close their literacy gap was the nature-based approach, which looks at brain differences along with socialization differences, to understand the overlapping and also sometimes contradictory learning styles of boys and girls. Kelley and her team applied the nature-based approach in tandem with organic alterations in teaching and learning environments, and closed a targeted boys' achievement gap while simultaneously raising girls' test scores. As Kelley has taught this approach around the world in the last six years, she has individualized and organized the approach into a leader's playbook, which she is sharing with you in these pages.

Third, Kelley's work with her team at Douglass showed the necessity of a school leader shepherding, organizing, advocating for, overseeing, and executing a powerful vision for school change in learning improvement for boys specifically. Boys need much more help in our culture than we realize, and Kelley is a dynamo—a team-building leader, a grassroots advocate for children, a gifted teacher, a clear organizer and delegator, and a social thinker who innovates from both within and without the systems she encounters. Her visionary eye is sharp, as you will see in this book; her leadership is practical and clear-headed. If she says a teacher can be trained to do something, she knows how to train that teacher. She understands how to provide gender balance, so that the needs of both boys and girls are met. She knows that educators are under immense pressure today, and she gives them tools by which to solve achievement gaps and release the pressure. Because so many of today's achievement gaps relate to boys' learning needs, she targets a crucial area of future progress for schools and communities.

Writing the Playbook can guide you to where you want to go as a leader, one step at a time, and Kelley and our whole Gurian Institute team walk with you, supporting you, throughout the journey. One of Kelley's first comments when I met her years ago was: "Change has to be immediate, but it also has to be sustainable. If it isn't sustainable, it is just flash-in-the-pan." How true this is. Enjoy this book not only for immediate practical strategies that can help you alter your school environment *today* but also for models of sustainability that will provide ongoing success for every child in your school.

Michael Gurian
Author of *The Minds of Boys* and *Boys and Girls Learn Differently!*

Preface

A child mis-educated is a child lost.

John F. Kennedy in a speech made to Congress in 1962

When little boys were being handed out, I got my son for a reason. I had been a teacher for eight years, and I had a lot to learn about boys. Connor taught me that little boys learn by smooshing, smearing, rolling, and colliding, and that not all boys want to sit on your lap and read. He taught me that some kids want to run around and hit things with big hammers and jump off of high places. He taught me that homework doesn't always get done at the kitchen table. Sometimes it gets done under it—or not at all. And he taught me that not all kids want to work hard enough to get an *A*. Some are perfectly satisfied with a *B* . . . or a *C*. I know you have met a boy like Connor. They make us scratch our heads, they test our patience, and they push us to get better at what we do. And that benefits all students—both boys and girls.

As a school principal, I had the opportunity to observe gender differences on a much larger scale. During the summer of 2004, as I dug through my school's data looking for achievement gaps between subgroups of students, I was shocked to see the extent of the gap between male and female achievement in reading and writing. Further analysis showed gaps in attitudinal and discipline data for boys as well. I knew that we had uncovered an area where, as a school, we were underserving many students, and where we had a huge lever-age point for overall school improvement. Through a collab-orative approach to goal setting, progress monitoring, and professional development, we armed ourselves with the avail-able research and operationalized our plan at all levels of the school. The "boy-friendly school" initiative that my faculty and I implemented yielded gap-closing results in just one year. Boys made eight times the expected gains in literacy, and girls made three times the expected gains. Students with dis-abilities made seven times the typical gains. Our overall school improvement rating shot up. With the right game plan, these results can be replicated.

This book is for educational leaders like you—building and district administrators, teacher leaders, instructional coaches, professional development directors, department chairs, and school board members—and for all those who want to get their hands on a leadership game plan for turning around the chronic low performance of boys in the PreK–12 educational system. With so many tasks competing for our attention in schools nowadays, this book gives you what you need—a straightforward, step-by-step playbook for launching your own yearlong or multiyear "boy-friendly" school initia-tive, including:

- The data you need to make the case with faculty, par-ents, district leadership, and other stakeholders;
- The science behind how the male brain learns;
- A school improvement plan that gets the whole team on board;
- Professional development tools and activities to sus-tain a multiyear focus;
- A look at well-intended school policies that hurt boys—and how we can fix these;
- Relationship-building tips that help boys feel that they really belong at school; and
- Classroom strategies that keep active boys engaged, motivated, and learning.

Written for school leaders by a school leader who has successfully closed the gender gap—and has helped many other school leaders do the same—this book does what no other book has done before. It brings together the topics of school leadership, brain science, and boys into one practical guide—your personal playbook for creating a boy-friendly (and a girl-friendly!) school.

Additional materials and resources related to *Writing the Playbook: A Practitioner's Guide to Creating a Boy-Friendly School* can be found at www.boyfriendlyschools.com. Kelley King can be reached at kelleykingpd@hotmail.com.

Acknowledgments

Many wonderful educators contributed their perspectives, insights, and activity ideas to bring this book alive. These special folks have been doing this work for years and are making a huge difference in the lives of boys. Your wisdom is so powerful. Thank you.

So many school-aged young men from across the country and beyond shared their brilliant perspectives on how to make schools more appealing. Your comments enlighten, inspire, and even stop us in our tracks. For your candor and willingness to speak, I thank you. I hope and pray that, through this book, I am an effective vehicle for delivering your message.

I am incredibly grateful for the contributions of two very special world-renowned experts and colleagues in this work— Michael Thompson and Ralph Fletcher. Even as you were busy writing and speaking on the topic of educating boys yourselves, you took time to collaborate with me. Thank you; I am truly in awe of your work.

The Gurian Institute has been my home for research and training and is an industry leader in developing best practices for gender-friendly classrooms. I thank the Gurian Institute certified trainers who contributed their invaluable perspectives to this book, and I thank Michael Gurian for inspiring us to keep moving forward.

If it hadn't been for Arnie Burvikovs, executive editor at Corwin, this book would never have been written. Thank you, Arnie, for seeking me out and for your encouragement. To

Kim, Desiree, Lauren, Cassandra, Terri Lee, Bryan, JJ, and the rest of the Corwin staff, thank you for all of your hard work on this book and for believing in the importance of my message.

PUBLISHER'S ACKNOWLEDGMENTS

Corwin would like to thank the following individuals for their editorial insight and guidance:

Judy Brunner, Clinical Faculty, Author, Consultant
Missouri State University & Instructional Solutions Groups
Springfield, Missouri

Dr. Virginia E. Kelsen, Principal
Rancho Cucamonga High School
Rancho Cucamonga, California

Dr. Alice Manus, Vice Principal of Academics, Guidance & Counseling
Soldan International Studies High School
St. Louis, Missouri

Tanna Nicely, Assistant Principal
Knox County Schools, Sarah Moore Greene Magnet School
Knoxville, Tennessee

Jonathan Wolfer, Principal
Douglass Elementary School
Boulder, Colorado

About the Author

Kelley King is a 25-year veteran educator, an international speaker, an author, and a mother of both a son and a daughter. As a Master Trainer for the Gurian Institute, Kelley travels widely to deliver keynotes, teacher workshops, and consultation to educators and parents. Additionally, Kelley develops and facilitates cutting-edge training curricula for online teacher education.

Kelley has worked at the elementary, middle, and high school levels in regular education, special education, and gifted and talented programs. She has served schools with diverse racial, linguistic, and socioeconomic student populations, as well as schools ranging from rural, one-room schoolhouses to large suburban schools. Kelley provides professional development in a wide range of private and public schools, including inner-city Title I schools across the United States. She has also had the privilege of working with teachers from Asia, the Middle East, Iceland, Canada, and Jamaica.

As a school administrator, Kelley led her staff to close the gender gap in reading and writing in just one year and, in doing so, gained national media attention. Kelley's work has been featured on *The Today Show*, National Public Radio, and *National Health Journal*, as well as in *Newsweek* magazine and in *Educational Leadership*. Kelley has coauthored (with Michael Gurian and Kathy Stevens) two previous books in the education field: *Strategies for Teaching Boys and Girls: Elementary Level* and *Strategies for Teaching Boys and Girls: Secondary Level*.

Making the Call

Is There Really a Boy Crisis?

Crisis: n. pl. **cri·ses** *a: An unstable or crucial time or state of affairs in which a decisive change is impending; a situation that has reached a critical phase.*

Merriam Webster's dictionary

You've picked up this book because you, like so many others, have a concern about the welfare of boys in school. As the mother of a son and a longtime educator myself, I share your concern. In every school, a disproportionate number of boys struggle to master basic literacy skills, sit on the bench outside the principal's office, get labeled hyperactive, and receive failing grades. Checked out, kicked out, or dropped out, too many boys—and especially boys of color and poverty—are failing to thrive in today's classrooms and schools. This is scary not only for boys but also for girls whose generation will be negatively affected by lower educational and employment levels of their male counterparts.

So does this amount to a crisis? Or is the problem being over-hyped? Whose fault is it? Does talking about boys hurt girls or diminish the importance of their needs somehow? These questions were first addressed by Michael Gurian, a pioneer in the study of gender, in his landmark book *The Wonder of Boys* (1997). With the release of the 2006 *Newsweek* story called "The Trouble With Boys" (Tyre, 2006), in which my school, Douglass Elementary, was featured, the debate continued to gain momentum and national attention. As experts polarized themselves on the issue of what we should call this problem, the trend data for boys continued its downward slide. The case is now closed on the matter. We can't turn a blind eye to this crisis. We need to roll up our sleeves and reverse these frightening trends now.

> Anyone in education who thinks our boys are not in crisis is misguided. As a mother, I could see the progressive descent into sorrow in my boys' posture: increasingly stooped, bent . . . "defeated." I don't think it serves anyone to beat ourselves up about not having met boys' needs at school in the past. Brain science and gender studies have grown by leaps and bounds over the last few decades. Now that we know better, let's do better!
>
> Sandy Lubert, mother of three boys and a teacher

Girls' underachievement in math and science has been an important part of the education conversation for some time—and rightly so. Initiatives focused on girls' achievement have been successful over time and warrant continued attention. The Center on Education Policy's 2010 report on boys' and girls' achievement finds: "In general, our analyses of performance by gender on state tests found good news for girls but bad news for boys. In math, girls are doing roughly as well as boys, and the differences that do exist in some states are small and show no clear national pattern favoring boys or girls."

From an international perspective, research led by Paola Sapienza (Guiso, Monte, Sapienza, & Zingales, 2008) at Northwestern University shows that, in societies offering equal educational opportunities to girls, the gender gap in math closes. The authors go on to report that, in every single country tested, girls score substantially higher in reading than boys do. The Center on Education Policy's results are consistent: In the United States in reading, boys are lagging behind girls in all states with adequate data, and these gaps are greater than 10 percentage points in some states. These analyses of state and international test results suggest that the most pressing issue related to gender gaps is the lagging performance of boys in literacy. Overlay gender gaps with those gaps associated with racial/ethnic and income subgroups, and the issue reaches alarming proportions.

How does all of this apply to your corner of the world? Most of the school-based trends for males that I've been referring to (and will discuss in greater detail later in this chapter) are universal across all groups. In fact, when I provide professional development in a school, I can pretty much sum up their challenges with boys before I even walk in the door! Reflect on these questions as they relate to your own educational organization:

> Back in the early '70s, schools became acutely aware that girls were behind in math and science and college admissions. That awareness prompted principals to search for young women science and math teachers, to work on programs that would help girls in math. It worked. Girls closed the gap in math and science. We now need the same effort with boys and writing. New focus, new approaches, not more of the same.
>
> Michael Thompson, PhD, coauthor of *Raising Cain: Protecting the Emotional Life of Boys*, and school psychologist

- Is the gender gap between boys' and girls' literacy/language arts scores pushing 10 points (or more)?
- Is boys' underachievement depressing your school's overall academic performance rating?
- Is it a crisis when an 8-year-old child who is below grade level in reading will most likely never catch up?
- Do the boys in your school earn more than 50% of the Ds and Fs and receive the majority of behavior referrals?
- Do boys make up the bulk of your noncompleters and dropouts?

- Is your school referring and staffing more boys than girls into special education?

This conversation—and this book—is not just for the sake of boys. Just as the success of girls is important for society as a whole, the success of boys is equally of value. When boys thrive, both boys and girls benefit. In my own school, girls made three times the expected gains in literacy when we implemented strategies to address the needs of boys. Educational achievement is not a zero-sum game. Dog-ear this page and come back to this section. This language may be just what you need as you talk with teachers, parents, and the community. It will be critical that you, as a change agent, be persuasive and compelling in creating a sense of urgency to do this work. Stakeholders must see that doing this work takes nothing away from girls because, as we will explore later, when we implement so-called "boy-friendly" strategies, the girls flourish as well. The time is now. Another generation of boys cannot afford to wait. So, now it is time for you to decide—is there a boy crisis?

> How do we systemically stop that flow of dropouts? We have to cut that spigot off at the preschool level.
>
> Leslie Block, PhD, consultant, Leslie S. Block & Associates

ACADEMIC ACHIEVEMENT

- Boys are 30% more likely than girls to flunk or drop out of school;
- Boys are almost twice as likely to repeat a grade;
- At the end of 12th grade, 26% of boys are below basic in writing compared to 11% of girls;
- In reading at the end of 12th grade, one-third of males are below basic compared to 22% of females;
- The underperformance of 17-year-old boys in reading is equivalent to 1.5 years of schooling;
- At the fourth and eighth grades, very similar gender gaps occur in both reading and writing;
- In 2005, females' average GPA was 3.09 while males' was 2.86;

- In 2006, the median girl was 17 percentile points in class rank above the median boy;
- Three times as many boys as girls say they do no homework;
- Thirty percent of boys say they usually or often go to school unprepared;
- By kindergarten, one in four black boys believes that he will fail in school;
- At the end of 12th grade, 42% of black boys fall far below basic in writing compared to 21% of black girls
- Fifty-five percent of black boys in high school are at risk of being off course or are off course for graduation;
- Almost one in four black boys is chronically absent; and
- When it comes to grades and homework, girls outperform boys in elementary, secondary, high school, college, and even graduate school.

Special Education

- Seventy percent of students in special education are boys;
- Boys make up 76% of students diagnosed with emotional disabilities and are three times as likely to be labeled conduct disordered;
- Learning disabled students are 73% male;
- Boys are four to five times more likely than girls to be diagnosed with attention deficit hyperactivity disorder (ADHD); and
- Black males between the ages of 6 and 21 are more likely to be labeled as mentally retarded and learning disabled and less likely to be in programs for the gifted than are white boys.

> If a boy is undereducated, too often the first thought is to refer him for special education. Interventions come too late for many boys and are not diagnostic, specific, or monitored.
>
> High school vice principal, Los Angeles Unified School District

Discipline

- Males are twice as likely to be suspended as females;
- Black males are six times as likely to be suspended as white males;
- In order from most frequently suspended to least frequently suspended: black males, white males, black females, white females;
- Males are 4.5 times as likely to be expelled as females;
- Males are more than four times as likely as girls to be referred to the office; and
- Males receive corporal punishment four times as often as girls.

(Continued)

(Continued)

Participation in Clubs/Activities

- Girls are over 1.6 times more likely to be involved in student council and student government;
- Girls are almost twice as likely to be involved in academic clubs;
- Membership in academic honor societies are 2-to-1 girls; and
- Athletics is the only extracurricular activity where boys' participation exceeds that of girls.

> We are losing our boys, turning out many young men without motivation and confidence. You have the ability to change this trend now and make your school a boy-friendly place where both boys and girls can find mastery and thrive.
>
> Betsy Hoke, retired school principal

College & Beyond

- Fifty-four percent of female sophomores are taking a college preparatory curriculum in high school compared to just 48% of males;
- Fewer than 30% of black boys in New York City graduated in 2011 with a Regents diploma, which is the diploma that indicates college readiness;
- Three-fourths of girls go on to college versus two-thirds of boys;
- Females are 1.5 times more likely to graduate from college (this is the opposite of the Baby Boomer generation, for whom 1.5 times more males than females graduated);
- Among blacks and Hispanics, women are more than twice as likely to earn college degrees than their male counterparts;
- According to 2008 U.S. Census Bureau data, young single women who are childless outearn their male counterparts in 39 of the 50 biggest cities in the United States and match them in another 8;
- Only one-third of black males under the age of 25 is employed;
- One in three black boys will do time in jail; and
- African American males make up only 6% of the U.S. population but make up more than 50% of the prison population.

Sources for statistics: Chaplin & Klasik, 2006; Greene & Winters, 2006; Gurian & Stevens, 2007; Kleinfeld, 2009; Losen & Orfield, 2002; Luscombe, 2010; Noguera, 2008; Payne & Slocumb, 2011; Planty et al., 2007; Schott Foundation, 2006; Sciutto, Nolfi, & Bluhm, 2004; Slocumb, 2004; Urban Studies Council, 2012.

THE FINAL BUZZER

The current statistics for boys and young men demand the attention of not only educators but also policymakers, legislators, and everyday citizens. If we don't reverse trends now, we risk raising a generation of men who do not fulfill their educational and employment potential.

> We have to find a hook for these boys so that they can really dial in. If school doesn't hook them, guess what's going to hook them?
>
> Leslie Block, PhD, consultant, Leslie S. Block & Associates

- Don't get caught up in the media debate about whether or not boys' problems rise to the level of a "crisis." Instead, take responsibility for the students in your school—dig up the data and reverse the downward trends for your boys.
- The education community has made great strides helping girls in the areas of math and science. Continue this important work and be empowered to seek the same improvements for boys in literacy, language arts, and college preparedness.
- As you educate staff members, parents, board members, and community members at large, share data from this chapter. Many people in our communities are unaware of the extent of these alarming trends. Let the data speak for itself and create a sense of urgency in your community.

Look around—How are the boys in your school doing? Are there areas where your boys are underperforming? What do the boys tell you about their school experience?

Warren Blair, principal, Wheat Ridge Middle School

 Additional materials and resources related to *Writing the Playbook: A Practitioner's Guide to Creating a Boy-Friendly School* can be found at www.boyfriendlyschools.com. Kelley King can be reached at kelleykingpd@hotmail.com.

Getting Your Head in the Game

"Need-to-Knows" About the Male Brain

Close your eyes, Have no fear, The monster's gone, He's on the run and your daddy's here, Beautiful, Beautiful, beautiful, Beautiful Boy.

John Lennon, from *Beautiful Boy (Darling Boy)*

A few years ago, I was on the phone conducting a radio interview about male and female brain differences. As I listened to the other guest on the show speak, it took everything I had to stay seated with the phone to my ear. "There are no biological differences between the male and female brain," the other guest (a university professor) was saying. "Furthermore, we are doing children a disservice to say that there are any differences. The brains of boys and girls are the same." Wow. My (female) brain swirled—where do I even start with this? Can she really believe this? I challenged her to stand up in a ballroom packed with teachers or in a school gymnasium full of parents and make that statement with a straight face. How someone could summarily dismiss decades of research and parent and teacher wisdom in one perfunctory statement was astounding to me. How could anyone logically assume that sex differentiation exists *only from the neck down?*

Oftentimes, this staunch position in favor of "no differences" (even in the face of what we know and experience every day), is fear based. How unfortunate that we should have to ignore the massive body of work documenting gender-based brain differences in the last 20 years. In fact, there are many examples of how failing to recognize differences has cost lives! Consider the field of medicine: prescriptions that work for males, don't work for females—or are even deadly. Women may have a heart attack and not realize it. Why? Because women have been taught to watch for a man's symptoms. We cannot continue to ignore (or refuse to acknowledge) that differences exist and deserve consideration in our work with boys and girls.

While this is a conversation about differences, it is *not* a conversation about better or worse. Rather, this is a conversation about brain specializations—some that occur more often in males (but not exclusively in males) and some that occur more often in females (but not exclusively in females). There is a great deal of overlap between the sexes and a lot of variation within each sex (Baron-Cohen, 2002). Thank goodness that, as educators, we have the wisdom to know that nothing is black-and-white, there is no one-size-fits-all to anything, and that we must teach to the learning styles

> Just because boys are wired differently than girls does not mean that they need to adjust to fit a largely female-based educational system. The system needs to adapt to reach every student and to capitalize on their strengths and interests.
>
> Mike Keppler, principal, Niwot Elementary School

of a diverse range of children—whose gender, by the way, is no small matter!

So where do we go from here? Well, now it's time to connect the dots. We know the statistics. You probably have already looked at your own school organization's statistics and that's why you have picked up this book. As educators, we know from experience that our boys are faltering in many areas, and we know that they approach school and life differently than our female students. We've identified the problem; now we need to find solutions. As a teacher and principal myself, I had a long-held understanding of the role of nurture in kids' development. Many years later, when I realized the extent of my school's gender gap, I began to study Michael Gurian's nature-based theory and realized that this was a missing piece. Equipped with both the science and the strategies, my faculty and I developed a clear a vision for where we needed to go. Before we can leap straight to the answers (I know it is tempting!), we have to let the brain be our guide. Let's take a peek under the hood and figure out—what makes the boy brain tick?

As you read this chapter, I imagine that you will experience more than a few "aha!" moments. Especially if you are a female-brained, female educator, it may be even harder for you to relate to the male experience in the classroom. I hope to shed some light. This is not a graduate course in brain science by any means, but it is certainly a wealth of information for any educator—information that we should all have if we are to be in the business of educating minds. I'll pay special attention to the characteristics and functioning of the male brain and will share a few practical and very important jewels of

> It is very important that we understand what makes these boys function. How do they think? What makes them be who they are? Why do they think that way? If we are going to be in the business of developing young men, then we need to gain every advantage in assisting them to develop in every facet.
>
> Edward Ybarra, principal, Central Catholic High School

knowledge—the *"So Whats?"* These best practices are well documented in the research, they apply across all grade levels, and they are what yielded unprecedented results for boys in my own school. Note that a more detailed discussion of the practical strategies (along with citations for use in your school improvement plan and for future study) can be found in Chapters 6 and 7.

> Over the past 20 years, I have observed that boys are having an increasingly difficult time thriving in schools, including the Montessori school that I led. Their motivation has decreased while their activity level has made it difficult for them to focus, learn, and complete work. My son struggled in school even though he had wonderful teachers. Some of them didn't understand boys and how to engage and enhance their motivation.
>
> Betsy Hoke, retired principal

LAYING THE GROUNDWORK

No wonder humans are curious about the brain! It is the organ of learning, and it has been—and still is—shrouded in a great deal of mystery. As educators, we are constantly seeking the right key to unlock this human equivalent of the "black box" and to maximize the learning capacity of each child's brain. It's an exciting time: Every day, scientists are learning more about the brain, and educators are able to put more and more brain-based instruction into place. Neuroscientists are still far from putting all the pieces together related to sex differentiation in the brain. Nevertheless, the research that has been conducted to date clearly demonstrates the existence of some important structural, chemical, and processing differences—small differences that, when combined with how we socialize children, turn into big differences in the classroom. While scientists are not always clear on how to translate their findings into specific classroom practice, there is widespread agreement that we cannot continue to teach almost exclusively to female learning styles and expect boys to learn equally well.

Finally, let me clarify something very important to this conversation about male and female brains. There are lots and lots of individual exceptions to any generalization; however—and this is key—*Exceptions do not disprove or invalidate the generalization.* Let's take height as an example. On average, men are taller than women; however, there are many women who are taller than the average man, and there are many men who are shorter than the average woman. Despite these many exceptions, the generalization is still true—men, on average, are taller than women. When applied to the science of the gendered brain, we know that not all males have strong male brains, just as not all females have strong female brains. Nevertheless, the generalization still stands: Men are more likely to be male brained, and females are more likely to be female brained.

Why Do These Sex Differences Exist?

During the course of human history, we have had different reproductive functions and have faced different selection pressures. As a result, sex differences exist. Males have historically had the role of inventing and making tools and weapons, as well as tracking and hunting animals. These activities required mechanistic, kinesthetic skills. Hunting requires the ability to track objects moving through space at a distance with good depth perception and strong eye-hand coordination. Having a single-minded focus and aggressive qualities also helped our male ancestors in the pursuit of prey (Baron-Cohen, 2002).

Females, on the other hand, have been the primary care-givers of children in every society of the world, past and present. This necessitated the development of verbal, social, and empathy skills associated with mothering and interacting with other females, sometimes in close quarters with multi-generational family groupings. Better visual acuity up-close and in dim lighting helped our female ancestors function better in sheltered settings. A more sensitive sense of taste and smell helped females select safe foods to eat. Better ability to hear high-pitched sounds gave females greater acuity to discriminate their own baby's cry and the type of cry (Baron-Cohen, 2002).

Nowadays, males (and females!) do not get enough opportunity to be in the environment for which they were designed—out in nature, exposed to sunlight and fresh air, with the ability to move in many different ways throughout the day. For boys, especially, this is neurologically challenging. Boys have been "brought in from the hunt," so to speak, to spend many hours a day in "the cave"—the verbal, auditory, affiliative, fine-motor environment that is the classroom of today.

OUR BEGINNINGS

Upon conception, the fetus is in the default setting of female regardless of whether the sex chromosomes are XX (female) or XY (male). At approximately five to six weeks in utero, the Y (male) chromosome triggers the mother's ovaries to release a testosterone surge. This testosterone surge marks the beginning of the sex differentiation process. Muscle mass, bone density, and hair follicle distribution are all influenced. The testes form and serve to sustain the testosterone surge. Becoming a male, then, requires extra developmental steps in utero—and more developmental steps create more opportunity for things to go wrong. In fact, more male fetuses are miscarried and stillborn or have sex-linked genetic disorders (Thompson & Barker, 2008). Males are also more vulnerable to X chromosome abnormalities. Color blindness is an example of this. If the X chromosome does not have the red and green receptor gene, the male will be color blind. Females on the other hand have two X chromosomes so if one of the X chromosomes is normal, it will provide the female with the ability to see reds and greens (Hanlon, Thatcher, & Cline, 1999; Lenroot et al., 2007).

The "testosterone bath" that predominates from five weeks to five months in utero also influences the brain. In the default setting, the fetus's female brain is wired entirely for language processing. The testosterone rewires some of these brain areas for visual-spatial-mechanical kinds of thinking. Both males and females receive testosterone in utero, but males receive more (Thompson & Barker, 2008). The amount of testosterone that any one of us received in utero had an instrumental role in designing our learning styles and preferences. More testosterone means a greater proportion of the brain was wired for spatial thinking (what is often called a "male brain"). Less testosterone means a greater proportion of the brain's language processing centers remained intact (a "female brain"). We all possess a unique ratio of verbal and spatial cortical areas that ultimately influences our placement on the continuum of male or female brainedness (Gurian & Stevens, 2010).

DOES THAT MEAN THAT OUR ABILITIES ARE FIXED?

"The ability for change is phenomenal. That's what the brain does best," says Dr. Jay Giedd (n.d.) of Temple University. In response to hormones, encouragement, practice, and diet, the brain is constantly changing. Biology and environment interact, and, in fact, if we want to ensure that biological differences don't become limitations, we must change the environment.

What all this boils down to is that there are advantages and disadvantages to every human being's brain; however, brains are not preprogrammed for life. Brain plasticity is the theory that addresses how the

> Helpful Tip: The phenomenon of brain plasticity is nicely explained in a children's picture book called *Your Fantastic, Elastic Brain: Stretch It, Shape It* by Joann Deak and Sarah Ackerley (2010). It can be used effectively at all levels, including high school. The book is a great tool for teaching students about their brains and their potential for actually growing their brains—"Just like lifting weights helps your muscles get stronger, learning new things strengthens your brain."

brain adapts to its environment—sort of a "use it or lose it" proposition. One small study showed that individuals who practiced juggling intensively increased gray matter in the corresponding area of their brain. When they stopped juggling, the gray matter disappeared (Draganski et al., 2004). A study of women playing the computer game Tetris over 10 weeks showed improvement in their spatial ability to the point that they could easily beat a strong male-brained man who had not been playing the game. If the man and woman both practiced the game, however, the male consistently beat the female (Haier, Karama, Leyba, & Jung, 2009). The reverse applies to males who can, with practice, improve "female-brained" skills like reading facial expressions.

THE MALE BRAIN 101

Corpus Callosum

The corpus callosum is like the Internet superhighway between the left and the right hemispheres. In females, the corpus callosum is larger in the back part of the brain where language representation occurs. This may contribute to females' advantages in earlier speech development and better auditory acuity for learning phonics (Baron-Cohen, 2004). Additionally, females have more neural connectivity in the corpus callosum, which predisposes the female brain to process information and use both hemispheres more quickly and efficiently. Males, on the other hand, tend to compartmentalize and lateralize brain activity, which means that they typically have a better single-task focus for greater lengths of time. More males are left-brained, while females have greater access to both sides (Cahill, 2005).

So What?

- Multisensory instruction helps stimulate more cortical areas in the brain (versus verbal alone), which helps the male brain stay more alert.

- Provide opportunities for boys to work on a single project for a longer time (versus changing gears frequently). Allow boys to explore a topic in-depth, versus only going for "breadth."
- Give more and earlier transitional cues for boys when it is time to switch gears. This may include a touch to the shoulder, flicking the lights, or playing music.

Limbic Size

The deep limbic system, responsible for bonding/nesting instincts, is larger in females than in males. This works both for and against women! As the result of hard wiring and socialization, females are generally more in touch with their feelings and better able to express their feelings. They enjoy more close friendships than do men and are generally more bonded and connected with others. On the other hand, females are more susceptible to emotional problems and mental illnesses, such as depression and anxiety. Smaller limbic size, in addition to how we socialize boys, explains why most boys need extra support in verbalizing their emotions. It also explains why boys are far less likely to carry a grudge (Brizendine, 2008, 2010).

So What?

- When boys are upset, let them cool off a bit before trying to talk with them.
- Have boys drink water regularly, especially when they are under stress. Walk and talk with a boy when it is time to debrief an emotional incident.

Frontal Lobe

The frontal lobes are sometimes called "The CEO of the Brain." It is an important area of the brain responsible for judgment, impulse control, and planning our behavior. Unfortunately, it is one of the last areas to develop. The frontal lobes of boys are slower to mature than girls. As a result, there is a greater propensity for risk taking and poor behavior choices, especially during adolescence (Brizendine, 2010; Giedd et al., 1999). Frontal lobe immaturity also reduces students' ability to delay gratification, to plan out their study time, to meet deadlines, to be motivated by grades that are "a long way off," and to stay organized.

So What?

- Insist that boys keep homework planners.
- Provide a structure for how boys should set up their binders.
- Do binder and desk checks regularly to ensure good organizational habits.
- Provide a place in the room where boys can turn in homework and pick up copies of assignments that they missed.
- Follow up with boys and don't let them slip through the cracks. Insist that they turn in their homework instead of skipping out on it (too many boys are fine with taking a zero in the grade book).
- Explicitly teach boys "how" to study, versus just telling them to study.
- Teach boys—even at high school—how to break up long-term projects into short-term deadlines. Do frequent checks along the way.

Hormones

Brain chemistry is powerful and influences all aspects of our brain's functioning. An article in *Cell* (Xu et al., 2012) compared hormones to the main electrical box on a house, "with many breaker switches, male and female behaviors are actually made up of many behaviors, like sex drive or an inclination to fight." Influenced both by biology and environment, hormones can fluctuate many times a day, reaching especially high levels during adolescence. The presence of these hormones influences behavior, motivation, and memory.

Testosterone is usually the first hormone that comes to mind when we talk about boys. Testosterone is associated with competitiveness, aggression, territorialism, assertiveness, and self-reliance (Hines, 2006). Increased testosterone enhances visual-spatial skills (high testosterone males and females do better on spatial tasks than their same-sex counterparts who have lower levels).

So What?

- Incorporate healthy competition into the classroom for boys.
- Understand that roughhousing is natural and normal (and actually enhances emotional, social, intellectual, and physical development in children).
- Give fidgety boys the opportunity to burn off excess energy through movement. Don't make them stop moving; rather, give them appropriate outlets or substitutions to satisfy their movement needs.

Dopamine is a neurotransmitter that affects a variety of areas of human functioning. Too little dopamine causes sluggishness and lack of coordination; too much causes fidgetiness and extraneous movement, such as tics. Dopamine levels are also connected to reward-seeking behavior, as well as impulse control and risk taking (Mandal, 2012). Boys are more likely than girls to get overexcited and have difficulty settling themselves back down. For example, if boys get really wound up playing a game in class, it can be harder and take longer for them to transition back to a quiet activity.

So What?

- Have boys "check in" with themselves by putting one hand on their heart and one hand on their stomach. Have them concentrate on breathing slowly.
- Play calming music to signal transitions.

- Always explain expectations (boundaries!) before an exciting activity, give feedback on how they do, and follow through with consequences for those who don't comply.
- Use a stopwatch and have students "beat the clock" to get back to their seats.

Serotonin is a neurotransmitter that is present in the central nervous system and in the digestive system. It influences a variety of functions, including sleep, mood, memory, muscle contraction, cognition, and memory. One way to describe serotonin's function is as the "volume control" of the brain. It influences the way that other signals in the brain are transmitted (Walderhaug et al., 2007). Too much serotonin leads to excess relaxation and sedation. Too little serotonin can lead to depression or poor mood in girls and impulsivity in boys (Walderhaug et al., 2007). Boys have less serotonin than girls and process it less effectively. As a result, boys may have greater difficulty settling down in the classroom.

So What?

- Incorporate team-building, feel-good activities in the classroom, which can enhance mood by increasing serotonin levels.
- Practice "Random Acts of Kindness"—serotonin levels rise when you help another person or observe an act of kindness.
- Teach boys self-calming strategies for use when they are upset, such as drinking water, deep breathing, or going for a walk.

Oxytocin is the primary human bonding neurotransmitter in the brain. It drives our desire to please and look good in the eyes of others. Oxytocin has a calming effect on the body and brain that helps us tolerate monotony and reduce fidgetiness. Guess what? Girls have more oxytocin than boys, leading boys to question authority more often, to be more fidgety, and to become bored in class more quickly (Brizendine, 2010).

So What?

- Help boys see the relevance of what they are learning by connecting the lesson objectives to their interest areas and to real-world applications.
- Give fidgety boys something to do with their hands, such as squeezing a stress ball or allowing them to stand up and move frequently.
- Team-building activities and doing things to help others increase oxytocin in the system naturally.

Spatial Processing

On tests of spatial functioning, males do better than females (remembering, of course, that not *all* males do better than *all* females, right?). As a generalization, though, we can say that males, on average, perform certain tasks such as mentally rotating objects in space and reading maps better than do females. Men process spatial tasks mostly in the right hemisphere (Alivisatos & Petrides, 1997) while women process these same activities bilaterally (Richter, Ugurbil, Georgopoulos, & Kim, 1997). What is interesting is that more difficult spatial tasks requiring a greater concentrated focus benefit from more localized processing, such as that which occurs in the male brain (OECD, n.d.).

So What?

- Provide multisensory (including visual), hands-on, experiential instruction to the greatest degree possible— and especially in literacy.
- Engage boys' bodies with their minds. Have boys learn and review concepts by incorporating movement and allowing their bodies to move through space.

Language Processing

Two key regions of the brain used for language—the Broca's and Wernicke's areas—are proportionally larger in the female brain (OECD, n.d.). In these regions, female brains are more densely packed with neurons, and the dendrites are longer. In addition to structural differences, there are processing differences. Females process language almost equally in both hemispheres of the brain. Males process language almost entirely in the left hemisphere. Difficult verbal tasks benefit from bilateral processing such as the female brain demonstrates. Females, on average, score better on tests of language ability than do males. A very interesting research report in the *Journal of Child Psychology and Psychiatry* (Whitehouse et al., 2012) shows that higher-than-normal levels of testosterone in utero is associated with a 250% increase in boys' chance of having a significant language delay by the age of 3. On average, boys are 1 to 1.5 years behind girls in receptive and expressive language development by the time they enter kindergarten (Ready, LoGerfo, Burkham, & Lee, 2005).

So What?

- Incorporate visual-spatial tasks into your literacy program, including drawing, pantomime, drama, and more.
- Allow boys to doodle, chew gum, or squeeze a stress ball while listening to read-alouds.
- Help boys develop an emotional vocabulary (feeling words), as well as an academic vocabulary.
- Play language games and incorporate read-alouds, even at the upper grades.

Memory

Your memory of an event is not stored in one location. Rather, various aspects of an event, such as the visual images, the sounds, the feelings, and the location, are stored in different areas of the brain that are responsible for those types of information. When you recall the event, you have to reconstruct the memory by drawing from multiple parts of the brain. This may be why females are better at remembering experiences, called "episodic memory." Boys, on the other hand, have better memory for disconnected facts—trivia, for example (Herlitz & Rehnman, 2008). In school, boys may be able to recall the facts of a story, but they may have greater difficulty recalling and explaining its theme. Additionally, memory is dynamic. That is, it decays naturally over time as new experiences and memories squeeze out the old ones. Fortunately, this natural decay can be reduced by incorporating a variety of rehearsal strategies that involve many regions of the brain.

So What?

- Have boys sketch out a memory before you have them write about it. This can help them "fill in some gaps" and end up with more detailed writing.
- Practice learning through visualizing, singing, mindmapping, role-playing, and with mnemonic devices.
- Have boys sketch a picture of what they are hearing while you do a read-aloud or while you lecture.
- During direct instruction, incorporate frequent opportunities for boys to turn to a neighbor and summarize what they just learned.

Stress

Interesting new research from the Prince Henry's Institute in Melbourne (Lee & Harley, 2012) is shedding some new light on male and female aggression responses due to stress. A specific gene found only on the Y chromosome (and responsible for the formation of the testes), called SRY, has a role in priming the male body for stress through increased blood flow to the organs and increased aggression and movement associated with the fight-or-flight response. Scientists have also found higher levels of fluid in the male spinal column, which allows the stress signal to travel more rapidly from the brain to the body, enabling males to activate a physical response more quickly. Females are more likely to adopt a less aggressive, tend-and-befriend response to stress.

So What?

- Don't ask a boy "What were you thinking?" right after an emotional or stressful incident. He wasn't thinking. He was reacting.
- Allow boys time to cool off after a stressful incident, such as a fight, and drink water to reduce stress.
- When it's time to talk, go for a walk. The physical movement lowers stress and increases blood flow to the brain.
- Talk to boys privately. Do not lecture or punish them publicly. It will seriously damage the boy's trust in you if he is embarrassed in front of his peers (more on this issue in Chapter 5).
- Be aware that boys (especially young boys who have poor self-regulation) have much more difficulty inhibiting aggressive behavior than do girls.
- Emotion is dominant over cognition. Identify and help resolve student stress so attention can return to learning.
- Enjoy the fact that your boys will "get over it" more quickly than girls and are less likely to hold a grudge!

Attention Span

Generally speaking, boys have shorter attention spans than girls. Boys go into rest states ("zone out") more easily and more often than girls. Why is that? While boys are way overdiagnosed with attention deficit disorder, it is true that boys are twice as likely to have the disorder as girls (CDC, 2012). Verbal-only instruction does not engage boys' strengths in the kinesthetic and spatial realms and is, without a doubt, not a boy-friendly mode of teaching. With lower levels of serotonin and higher levels of testosterone, sitting still is neurologically harder for boys (James, 2007). And with lower levels of oxytocin, boys are more likely to ask the question, "Why do I have to do this?"

So What?

- Limit "sit-n-git" instruction for boys. Verbal-only instruction should be kept short and interspersed with frequent processing activities and movement opportunities.
- Give boys the opportunity to move a bit in their seats—encourage silent tapping on the thigh or squeezing a stress ball, for example.
- Allow boys to stand in the back of the room during lectures. Boys are more alert standing than sitting.

The Senses

Boys are more likely to be color blind (Montgomery, 2012). They have more trouble seeing things up-close and are better at seeing things at a distance. Their eyes are better equipped for bright outdoor light as opposed to dim lighting. Most boys are better at tracking objects moving through space than tracking small print across a page. In terms of hearing, boys do not hear high-pitched and soft sounds as well as girls, but they are better at localizing sound, perhaps because of the larger size of their head (our brains localize sound by judging the time it takes for the sound to travel from one ear to the other). Boys' hearing is also not as finely tuned to hearing phonemic differences, which is important to learning how to read (James, 2007).

So What?

- Boys will hear you better if your voice is louder and lower.
- Use more primary colors in the classroom and keep it simple—fewer pastels and less clutter.

- Be more dynamic in your teaching style—move around, gesture with your hands, etc. This catches the boy's eye, which is a "heat-seeking missile" for objects moving through space.
- Take boys outside for learning regularly. The natural outdoor light helps the development of their brain.

Maturation Timeline

There are differences not just in the structures and chemicals of the brain but also in the developmental timetable. Brain size in females peaks at about 11.5 years old in girls and about 3 years later in boys. The average girl is typically 1–1.5 years ahead of boys and complete development of the brain occurs in the early 20s for females and the late 20s to the early 30s for males (Giedd, 2004; Lenroot et al., 2007). Development of verbal fluency, handwriting, and the ability to recognize familiar faces also occurs earlier in girls. Boys, however, are 4–8 years ahead of girls in the development of mechanical reasoning, visual targeting, and spatial reasoning, according to researchers at Temple University (Giedd, 2004).

> Parents worry about their sons in school. They tell me stories like, "When he's writing, his pen may all of a sudden become a spaceship." I tell them, "Don't worry—your son is normal!"
>
> Vermelle Greene, principal/founder (retired), SACRED Life Boys Academy

So What?

- Upper elementary, middle, and high school students need developmentally appropriate, multisensory, hands-on instruction. This isn't just for the primary grades!
- Use less lecture and more hands-on, socially interactive, experiential, and active learning.

Is There Such a Thing as an "Extreme Male Brain"?

Simon Baron-Cohen is a well-known researcher of the brain, including gender differences in the brain. While most people have sex-typical brains in the average or moderate range, he notes that some people have extremely strong or weak versions. He compares it to height differences—most people are average, but some people are exceptionally tall or exceptionally short. Given that the average male brain is a "systemizing/mechanistic" brain, what is an "extreme male brain"? Baron-Cohen (2004) suggests that the extreme male shares the same characteristics as autism. Individuals diagnosed with autism tend to be blind to other people's minds or emotions. Autistics also tend to assume that other people think exactly as they do. Interestingly, four out of five people with autism are males.

The Male Adolescent Brain

Many people think that the brain finishes its development around age 18—wrong! Brain development is only about 80% complete at that age (Baird & Bennett, 2006). Because the brain develops from the back to the front, the frontal lobes—the part of the brain responsible for judgment, evaluating risk, delaying gratification, and planning ahead—are the last to develop. Complicating matters, the frontal lobes develop later in boys than in girls. Males have higher levels of the aggression and sex hormone, testosterone, and a stronger urge to act out physically when under stress. Additionally, the male brain is more sensitive to the neurotransmitter dopamine and, therefore, receives greater pleasure sensation from the "rush" of taking risks. All of these factors conspire to form the mind of the teen male that seeks three things—pleasure, novelty, and danger (Brizendine, 2010).

It's important for high school teachers to remember that the young men in their classrooms have brains that are more like a child's than like an adult's. Yes, those boys may be big and hairy and smelly, but their adult bodies do not house adult brains. Many high schools use lecture as the primary teaching method. This is not an effective style for young men, just as it is not an effective style for young boys. In fact, lecture is not the most effective teaching method for anyone of any age.

For more information about adolescent brain development, you may want to visit the "Young Adult Development Project" website (http://hrweb.mit.edu/worklife/young adult/index.html). It is a wonderfully comprehensive resource for further exploration of adolescent issues.

It's Nature *and* Nurture!

It always fascinates me how basic male-female brain differences manifest themselves in very similar ways, regardless of race, ethnicity, nationality, language background, socioeconomic status, and—perhaps most telling—culture. Teachers have many of the very same "boy" observations and "boy" questions, while struggling to turnaround the same underachievement trends that the international research bears out. In fact, the old "Nature or Nurture" argument seems almost silly. We are not solely products of our environment or products of biology. We are products of both!

The Final Buzzer

Research over the past 30 years has shown a number of structural, chemical, and processing differences between the male and female brain. As educators, we must work diligently and ethically to understand both the biological and sociological variables that mold our children's learning styles and then differentiate instruction accordingly.

- Sex differences emerged in response to different survival pressures over the history of man.
- Sex differentiation begins in utero. Testosterone takes center stage in molding the male body and mind.
- Learning about specific sex differences in the brain helps educators identify a number of critical strategies to ensure success, both academically and behaviorally, for boys.
- The brain does not finish its development in adolescence. Young men need to be taught in developmentally appropriate and boy-friendly ways.
- Experience shapes the brain, which means that we are products of both nature and nurture.

One of the best things in the world to be is a boy; it requires no experience, but needs some practice to be a good one.

Charles Dudley Warner

Additional materials and resources related to *Writing the Playbook: A Practitioner's Guide to Creating a Boy-Friendly School* can be found at www.boyfriendlyschools.com. Kelley King can be reached at kelleykingpd@hotmail.com.

Chalk Talk

A Game Plan for Moving
Your Team Down the Field

We continually brought the hard data to the table and asked questions. What are we asking of boys? What are we willing to do differently?

Larry Shores, principal, Winona Elementary School

When my former school, Douglass Elementary in Boulder, Colorado, was in the media spotlight for its success with boys, I was interviewed by a lot of reporters from all around the country. I was struck by how every interviewer wanted that convenient "nugget" of information—the straightforward, easy-to-implement strategy for turning around boys' achievement. Certainly, it would have been easy for me to rattle off a list of strategies disembodied from the context of our broader school improvement work together, but I would not have done the "boy-friendly" initiative justice. So, to tell the whole story of my school's success, I had to talk about the school culture and climate first.

What do gender differences have to do with school leadership? Everything! As school leaders leading a staff of men and women, we need to be masterful in providing effective leadership for both genders. Differences in how men and women communicate, negotiate, and solve problems can have a profound effect on a school's climate. For a wealth of information about gender-friendly leadership, check out Michael Gurian and Barbara Annis's book *Leadership and the Sexes: Using Gender Science to Create Success in Business* (2008).

Back then, as I spoke to reporters, and still today, I use this analogy about how it all fits together: It's springtime, and you are ready to plant your garden. You have two kinds of soil and two kinds of seeds with which to work. First, you take your best seeds (high levels of purity and germination) and plant them into soil that is of poor quality. The soil is dry, rocky, and lacking nutrients. It does not get optimal light, and it does not get sufficient moisture. Next, you take your lesser seeds—they are older, are less pure, and don't germinate as well—and plant them in well-prepared soil. This soil, by contrast, is rich in nutrients, has optimal pH levels, and is exposed to ideal light and moisture. The high-quality seeds in the poor soil conditions are slow to sprout, and their root system is weak. Most of these seeds do not germinate at all. The poor-quality seeds in the rich soil, however, perform much better with strong root systems. They grow and bear fruit.

The change we most need is a change in attitude and approach. Administrators and teachers have to be aware that boys are in trouble in school, that what we have been doing works well for girls and less well for boys.

Michael Thompson, educational consultant and author of *Raising Cain*

Now, think of the "seeds" as instructional strategies that are being planted in the "soil" of the school's culture and climate. As seeds need nutrients, our instructional strategies need a fertile environment that boasts high levels of trust, support for risk taking, and lots of faculty buy-in. Is the soil of your school nourishing? Can new ideas take root, or is growth met with resistance?

SCHOOL CULTURE AND CLIMATE—WHAT'S THE DIFFERENCE?

In education, one of our main priorities is to create a safe environment for students to learn. Because the brain gives priority to processing incoming data that may pose a threat to survival, emotion is dominant over cognition—that is, emotional safety must be present before the mind can turn to the tasks of learning and taking risks (Wolfe, 2011). The adults in our charge are no different. Without a safe environment, the adults' learning and willingness to take risks will also be inhibited. If we want to see change and improvement, we absolutely have to address this issue. No shortcuts. Remember—this is the soil, and we need to prepare it. Time spent doing this preliminary and ongoing work is time well spent.

Let's dissect this a bit. Sometimes we refer to this safe environment issue as the "culture" of the school, and sometimes we use the word "climate." Are they interchangeable? And if not, what's the distinction? A wonderful article on this topic was published in *Principal* (March/April 2008). From page 58: "[I]f culture is the personality of the organization, then climate represents that organization's attitude. It is much easier to change an organization's attitude (climate) than it is to change its personality (culture)" (Gruenert, 2008). Our personality is far less susceptible to change than our attitude.

When a whole school system has a collective response over time, this becomes part of the culture of the school. It is "the way we do things around here." Very often, the "way we do things" flies directly in the face of best practice when it comes to reaching and teaching male learners. Important questions to ask include:

- How does your school respond in the face of student disciplinary problems?
- What is the culture of your organization in terms of eschewing lecture for more active and engaging approaches?
- Does the culture of your organization respond to missed homework with zeroes or insist that the work get done, even if it's late?
- Do staff members, individually and collectively, have a positive attitude about working with boys?
- When your school describes the "ideal student," does that description sound more like a girl than a boy?
- How might your school's time-honored ways of doing things (your school's culture) be getting in the way of boys' success?

I have worked in schools and with teachers who embrace the characteristics and qualities of boys and, unfortunately, I've worked in places where the opposite is true. Recently, I worked in a coed school with gender-specific classes. I quickly discovered that—in the minds of the staff—teaching an all-boys class was like pulling the short straw. No one wanted to get stuck with that assignment. I felt so sad for those boys. Kids are perceptive, and too many boys already have a pretty good sense that they aren't a good fit for school. This was an example of a school's attitude (climate) toward boys that had become so widespread as to become the school's personality (culture) of negativity toward boys.

Let's now turn our attention to what you can do, as a school leader, to better understand and positively affect both the school's climate and its culture as it relates to working with boys. In the next section, I offer a number of tried-and-true activities that work well during Professional Learning Communities. You and your leadership team may choose to use a few or all of the activities as you customize a yearlong plan.

ACTIVITIES FOR YOUR PROFESSIONAL LEARNING COMMUNITIES

An essential part of understanding your school's climate and culture is to understand the *knowledge, attitudes, and beliefs* of the people in your school. The following group activities provide a number of ways to get teachers dialoguing, while giving you an opportunity to listen and learn. For the teachers themselves, these activities lay the critical groundwork for shifts in perception and the development of buy-in—both of which are critical to the improvement initiatives that lie ahead. Listen for themes of underlying resistance, fear, or concern related to specifically addressing boys' needs. Acknowledging these issues, and then looking at your school's gender data, can serve to honor individual perspectives while unifying the group around a call to action.

Note: The following Professional Learning Community (PLC) activities can be used with a variety of stakeholders (in fact, I encourage it!); however, for the sake of simplicity here, I refer to your audience as "teachers."

PLC Activity #1: Text Rendering

Start by providing a copy of the article "School Culture, School Climate: They Are Not the Same Thing" from *Principal* magazine (Gruenert, 2008). Have teachers discuss in small groups the climate and culture of their classrooms. With a school improvement focus on boys' engagement and achievement, challenge your educators to look through the lens of the boys' experiences. What *attitude* does your classroom exude toward boys? What is the *personality* of your classroom, and what is the effect on boys? Think of one of your most challenging male students: Can the staff make some conjectures about this boy's physical, social, emotional, and mental experience in the classroom? Engage male staff members in sharing their own school experiences. What sorts of school climates and cultures did they experience growing up?

PLC Activity #2: Brainstorming

Once my school had decided to tackle the boys' gender gap, one of the first conversations we had was one of our experiences and perceptions related to both boys and girls. It was both enlightening and funny. Try this: Have teachers sit in small groups. Vertical teams or mixed departments can be an enlightening way to group teachers for the discussion. Post the discussion prompt: "What do you enjoy about working with boys?" Allow participants to discuss and make a few notes. Follow this with the prompt: "What do you find challenging about working with boys?"

Following further small-group discussion, have people share their responses and make notes on a display. A pattern quickly emerges. Most of the things listed in the "enjoy" column also belong in the "challenges" column! The group might also observe that many of the boy strengths do not help them get good grades—in fact, they hurt their grades. If you do the same exercise related to girls, you'll see that girls have many characteristics that support getting good grades; however, their fragilities appear in the social-emotional domain ("drama" and "cliques" are common responses about the challenges of working with girls). Remind your faculty that these lists are generalizations and that there is overlap between boys and girls. The purpose of this activity, however, is to point out these differences to bring us to the all-important question: Are we recognizing and honoring the natural characteristics of both boys and girls?

A nice way to provide closure for this activity is to look at the list of boy characteristics and brainstorm how one can "harness" or tap into the competitiveness, creativity, out-of-the-box thinking, sense of humor, and other qualities that boys bring to the classroom. How can these qualities work *for* us, instead of against us, in the classroom? This perceptual shift (strength based versus deficit based) can provide a powerful starting point for changes in teachers' attitudes and perceptions about teaching boys.

PLC Activity #3: Root Cause Analysis

An activity that I learned during my time as a principal in the Boulder Valley School District is one that can be used as a discussion starter for any issue or question in a school. One can learn much about the culture of the school by listening to the teachers' discussions. I call this activity "Root Cause Analysis." This activity would also work very well early on in your conversations about addressing boys' needs—I suggest doing this *before* you develop the intervention strategies for your school improvement plan. As you are sharing and discussing national and school data, consider utilizing this activity.

Share with teachers the national and international data about boys' performance from Chapter 1. If you prefer, use your own school's data for this activity. Have teachers select one statistic and write this statistic at the top of a piece of chart paper. Have teachers then ask "Why?" For example, perhaps they have selected the statistic: Three times as many boys say that they do no homework. They write that statement and then ask themselves, "Why don't so many boys do homework?" Group members discuss, then decide on one possible cause. Perhaps they decide that boys don't find the homework very interesting. Then the group asks themselves, "Why don't boys find the homework to be interesting?" The group discusses and perhaps they decide that it is because homework is not relevant. They then ask themselves, "Why is homework not relevant to boys?" Continue this process with the group discussing and recording as they go. After 10–15 minutes of discussion, have the small groups share with the other groups either through brief presentations or through a Gallery Walk (posting charts on walls and allowing all groups to circulate and read).

I find it informative to see which statistics the groups select, as well as the direction of their conversations. Do most groups select statistics on discipline? Do your groups predominately select the literacy statistics or the substance abuse statistics? It is also interesting to see where participants go with their discussion. Do they perceive that the problems are caused by the students' home lives? Teaching methods? Lack of role models? Hardwired biology? While some of these issues are not within the "control" of the school, a surprising number of the issues are within the school's control. This then leads us to my next suggested group activity.

PLC Activity #4: Characteristics Web

In my work with one Colorado school on the issue of "reluctant writers" (most of whom are boys!), I had teachers draw a large circle on flip-chart paper and write "Characteristics of Reluctant Writers" in the center. This could be titled any way that best fits the focus of your discussion. For example, the web might have been titled "Characteristics of Male Learners" or "Characteristics of Boy Writers." From there, the teachers drew out many spokes and wrote down lots of different characteristics of reluctant writers.

As the next step, I had them go back and circle the characteristics that they, as teachers, could actually impact in the classroom. They were surprised that they could have an impact on almost every issue that they had identified. The visual display was eye-opening, probably because we are usually so quick to assume that things are out of our control, especially for highly impacted students. This activity can be a good one for generating ideas about classroom strategies and interventions. For this purpose, teachers can extend the activity by listing interventions next to the characteristics they circled. Have teachers do a Gallery Walk to view the other groups' ideas. After the meeting, have all the groups' webs mapped into one comprehensive map reflecting everyone's ideas. Figure 3.1 provides an example of a brainstorming web that teachers might create.

Figure 3.1 Characteristics Web

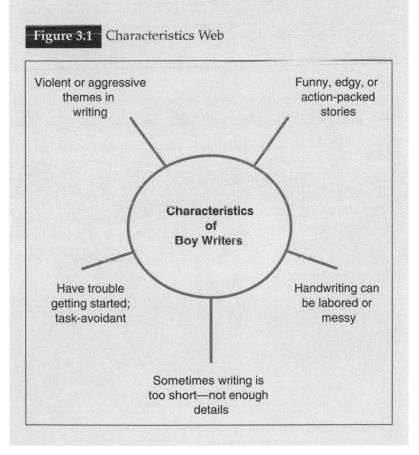

PLC Activity #5: Water/Gas/Electric Puzzle

The Water/Gas/Electric problem, otherwise known as the "Three Utilities" problem, can be effectively used just prior to a faculty/staff conversation about schoolwide policies and procedures that work for and against male learners (see Chapter 4). The activity's hands-on, visual-spatial, and collaborative nature gets everyone's brains alert and their energy into the room. In 2005, a guest presenter led this activity very effectively with my school and several others to get us thinking about self-imposed barriers to our own success. Perhaps you have come across this mathematical brain-teaser on the Internet; however, I would be very surprised if your teachers know the answer already.

Distribute flip-chart paper, markers, and sticky notes to groups of five to six teachers. Use visual displays and the following instructions to set up the activities in Figures 3.2 and 3.3.

Figure 3.2 Power Houses A & B

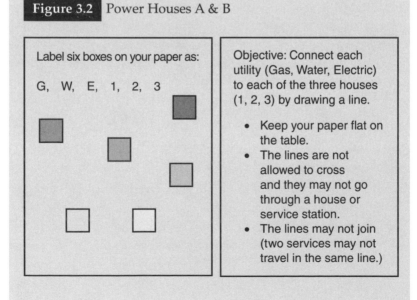

Label six boxes on your paper as:

G, W, E, 1, 2, 3

Objective: Connect each utility (Gas, Water, Electric) to each of the three houses (1, 2, 3) by drawing a line.

- Keep your paper flat on the table.
- The lines are not allowed to cross and they may not go through a house or service station.
- The lines may not join (two services may not travel in the same line.)

Allow the groups to work together for 10–15 minutes on finding a solution. Observe closely: Who takes charge of the group? Who sits back? Do some people start working on their own piece of scratch paper separate from the group? How persistent are the groups? Who gives up and pushes back from the table? Does anyone conclude that it can't be solved? Who "talks it through," and who prefers to draw in silence? Who wants to challenge the rules or creatively interpret them?

When you call them back together to see if anyone has solved the challenge, you have the unenviable task of telling them that the puzzle cannot be solved. It can't be solved, that is, with the given set of rules. This creates an opportunity for discussion, specifically, what are the key learnings for us as a school community? While a number of observations will be shared, perhaps the most important one is: *"Sometimes we make rules (or are faced with rules) that get in the way of solving problems."* Teachers will most certainly point out that they could have solved the Power Houses problem if they had been allowed to change just one rule! Great! So let's apply that to your work as a school staff: What "rules" (or policies/procedures) has your school organization created that are getting in your way? What things get in the way of boys' success? What changes would make success more attainable for boys?

Figure 3.3 Power Houses C

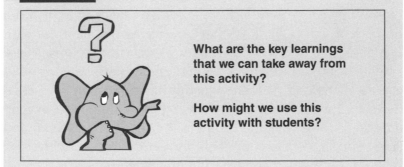

What are the key learnings that we can take away from this activity?

How might we use this activity with students?

Teachers can use this activity in their classrooms to learn about their students' personalities, learning styles, collaborative styles, and tolerance for frustration. Kids love it, and it spurs some great classroom discussion afterward.

Team Building

At all times of year and stages of a faculty's work together, I am a huge proponent of developing collaboration and collegiality on a staff in a systematic and ongoing way. Relationship building is key to helping everyone optimize their potential (and it belongs in the classrooms too!). This fun stuff makes the hard work much easier. It changes the climate, and it can shift the culture. And, most important, it is brain friendly to work and learn in this way. As principals and teacher leaders, be sure to practice what you preach whenever you have assembled a group of people. Make sure YOUR teaching and group facilitation are as brain friendly and as engaging as you are asking teachers to be with students.

Brain Boosters at Faculty Meetings

Assign a staff member (or a team/department) to lead a brief activity that gets everyone up and moving around. It could be as simple as "Share a celebration from your classroom with three other people in the room" or as silly as turning on some music and keeping a beach ball up in the air for 3 minutes (borrow some ideas from Chapter 7). Activities like this do a number of things. First, teachers are trying out activities with one another that can be used back in their classrooms. These activities are an essential component of any boy-friendly classroom. Second, activities like this have a positive impact on the participants' brains by increasing blood flow and oxygen (critical for attention and thinking), increasing dopamine and serotonin (for feelings of pleasure and positivity), and increasing oxytocin (for human bonding and attachment).

Helpful Resources

Here are a collection of resources to support team building and brain boosters with faculty:

- Cain, J., & Jolliff, B. (2010). *Teamwork and Teamplay: A Guide to Cooperative, Challenge, and Adventure Activities That Build Confidence, Cooperation, Teamwork, Creativity, Trust, Decision Making, Conflict Resolution, Resource Management, Communication, and Effective Feedback.* Dubuque, IA: Kendall Hunt Publishing.
- Cain, J., Anderson, M., Cavert, C., & Heck, T. (2010). *Teambuilding Puzzles: 100 Puzzles and Activities for Creating Teachable Moments in Creative Problem Solving, Consensus Building, Leadership, Exploring Diversity, Group Decision Making, Goal Setting, Active Learning, Communication & Teamwork.* Dubuque, IA: Kendall Hunt Publishing.
- Cain, J., Cummings, M., & Stanchfield, J. (2012). *A Teachable Moment: A Facilitator's Guide to Activities for Processing, Debriefing, Reviewing and Reflection.* Dubuque, IA: Kendall Hunt Publishing.
- Miller, B. C. (2004). *Quick Team-Building Activities for Busy Managers: 50 Exercises That Get Results in Just 15 Minutes.* New York, NY: AMACOM Books.
- Miller, B. C. (2008). *50 Quick Meeting Openers for Busy Managers.* New York, NY: AMACOM Books.

Got Data?

Although we can easily tire of all the required assessments nowadays, we might as well turn lemons into lemonade. Let's try to mine the data for what we can. The disaggregation of criterion-referenced tests, such as state assessments, can

> We let the data tell the story. Is what we are doing working? When we focus on what works for boys, our achievement and growth have improved for both boys and girls. When we move away from that focus, our achievement changes.
>
> Jonathan Wolfer, principal, Douglass Elementary School

give us a picture of achievement differences between boys and girls. Are there gaps in certain subject areas? Or at certain grade levels? Typically, girls are outperforming the boys by a small margin in reading and by a larger margin in writing. Are there sub-content areas where differences appear more strongly? What is the gender representation in the highest level of proficiency (i.e., above proficient or advanced)?

For an interesting rundown on the current state of the gender achievement gap, check out the Center for Education Policy's report on the status of the gender achievement gap (CEP, 2010). Consider having staff read the CEP report as well. I find it helpful to start with national, and even international, data and then bring it closer to home with state or provincial data, then district/regional data, and then school data to see if the larger trends mirror your own school's trends. Don't forget to also compare your own school to other "like schools," in terms of your student demographics.

Other data sources, such as assessment information from MAPS, Dibels, DRA2, and the like, can also be disaggregated. Have you disaggregated your kindergarten readiness and benchmark data by gender? Results for letter and sound identification, concepts about print, counting, and shape recognition will probably be very enlightening.

School personnel often overlook other sources of valuable information. I encourage you to disaggregate your data by gender related to grade point average, grades, behavior rankings on progress reports, attendance, special education (Response to Intervention) referrals, gifted and talented referrals and screening data, high school completion, and discipline. In terms of discipline, you can further track boys and girls according to the number, location, severity, and type of discipline incidents. Some schools have also tracked discipline referrals (type and number) by gender of the teacher and gender of the student. By doing this, schools can see if proportionately more discipline referrals are given by male or female teachers for any specific types of discipline and to either gender of student.

When teachers do the Root Cause Analysis activity (described earlier in this chapter), a frequent point of conversation is whether or not female teachers are less tolerant of boys' rambunctious behavior and, subsequently, give more discipline referrals to boys than do male teachers. If this conversation emerges (and it likely will), a perfect jumping-off point is created for the deeper exploration of discipline data at your school.

A Picture's Worth a Thousand Words

We receive voluminous tomes of data. How do we wade through it all and do it in an inclusive and collaborative way? Several years ago, in an effort to create more teacher involvement in data disaggregation from the ground up, I would have teachers break into groups to comb through the raw data and make some meaning of it themselves. But time, as always (and increasingly so with cuts in teacher preparation days in the fall), was limited. I wanted teachers to have time to get to the important work of developing improvement goals and intervention strategies and felt like part of the process was being rushed as we ran out of time.

At that point, I made a strategic shift that worked very well. During those summer days before teachers returned, I had access to the year-end data and started the process of looking for the big celebrations and challenges that jumped out at me. As the principal of the school, I had a unique "big picture" lens that individual teachers or parents didn't necessarily have. Principals have their finger on the pulse of individual students and teachers, while still having a balcony view of the organization. Therefore, I was able to knowledgeably jump back and forth in the data to spot trends for the school overall, as well as trends for grade levels/departments, individual teachers, and individual students.

> The data told the story. It was evident that we have a gender achievement gap and needed an intervention to close that gap.
>
> Kristie Venrick, principal, Blue Mountain Elementary School

It was then my task to "reduce background noise in the data," to bring the big issues forward, and, most important, to make meaning. While district data programs are getting better all the time at filtering data and creating visual displays, I still relied on creating many of my own charts due to the control it gave me. The charts were simple, straightforward, and easy to understand and clearly illustrated important trends that I wanted the faculty and staff to explore more deeply. In short, I wanted the charts to jump right off of the screen when stakeholders viewed them.

Viewing the data in a strong visual representation did a couple of things. It really shone a light on important issues, and it created a sense of urgency. I heard teachers make comments like, "Wow, we really have a gender gap in writing. We really need to address that!" Very quickly, it became the teachers' discovery that we had big gender achievement gaps, and it was their demand that we address them.

Getting Teacher Buy-In

Certainly, one look at the data will speak volumes to your staff; however, I want to also connect this issue of buy-in to the beliefs and attitudes each of us brings to the table. Across nationality, culture, race, socioeconomic, and language backgrounds, teachers share very similar concerns regarding their male students: "How do I get them to sit still long enough to actually get their work done?" "My boys just get so carried away! How do I get them focused?" "What can I do about boys who have no interest in the content?" and "How do I get boys to turn in their homework more reliably, or at all?" As a school leader, these concerns among teachers make our work easier.

> We used teacher-led training to facilitate the process of implementing gender-based instructional strategies. When stakeholders take ownership in their own learning and development, they will implement at a higher level of fidelity.
>
> Dr. Derrick Lowe, academy leader, B.E.S.T. Academy

In all of these cases, teachers will acknowledge that, generally speaking, their female students are having fewer problems in many school-related areas. The girls sit still for longer periods of time, tend to be more compliant, and are more likely to do (and turn in) their homework. Therefore, when we are ready to talk about issues of gender, teachers already "get it"—they have personal experience with gender (unlike poverty, learning problems, or other student variables with which they may have no life experience). And, I daresay, there is not a teacher in the room who doesn't see boys' qualities and characteristics as simultaneously heartwarming and downright frustrating.

Activities such as the Root Cause Analysis (and others described earlier in this chapter) lay the groundwork for exploring and changing perceptions about boys and schooling. Combined with a compelling portrayal of the gender gap data, the issues become blatantly obvious and more urgent for all. Additionally, connecting this work to your staff's personal lives increases personal relevancy and buy-in.

> I have yet to speak to a teacher who fails to see the good of understanding better the basis of boy behavior and how to manage it.
>
> Tim Coble, K–12 chair of world languages, American School of Doha

- Which of your staff members are parenting a boy?
- Has their own son struggled in school?
- Do they have a nephew or grandson who has struggled in school?
- Why did that boy struggle, and what could have been different about school to help these boys be more successful?

These questions make great fodder for small-group discussions. On both a professional level and a personal level, we can all connect to the importance—and urgency—of figuring out how to be more successful with boys.

> We began by asking teachers to observe how boys and girls learn and to discuss what they were noticing. This led them to see that how the instruction was often better suited to girls. The teachers with sons at home seemed to readily accept and understand these differences.
>
> Warren Blair, principal, Wheat Ridge Middle School

"Yes, but . . ."

Anticipating the objections is essential in our work as persuasive and effective change agents in our schools. One of the biggest objections, or at least questions, you may face is, "But what about the girls?" Sometimes teachers will say, "But boys seem to do okay out in the world, so why should we be so focused on them at school?"

There are two big myths in the above statement. First, things are a-changin' for boys in the world! If you haven't shared the statistics on college enrollment and degree completion, it's time to do it. And remember to point out that the balance isn't shifting just because girls are accomplishing more. It's shifting the most because boys are opting out of higher education (or are unprepared/unqualified to be admitted). Also, check out those salary statistics from Chapter 1 regarding single/childless female pay versus single/childless male pay. The underwhelming achievements of boys and young men are increasingly causing problems for young women who are having a harder time finding suitable mates—men who have the education levels and earning potential that they do.

> Some teachers expressed concern that we needed to keep our focus on girls performing well in school. Once teachers realized that the strategies were beneficial to all learners, they really got behind the changes.
>
> Mike Keppler, principal, Niwot Elementary School
>
> As a principal, I did not have to persuade my teachers. We simply had deep conversation about our data and the staff wanted to seek additional strategies to address the gender achievement gap.
>
> Cathy O'Donnell, principal, Blue Mountain Elementary School

The second myth is that we are focusing on boys at the expense of girls. Wrong! This is not a zero-sum game. For better or worse, boys push the envelope when it comes to teaching and classroom management. The challenges they present require us to think more creatively about how to engage and motivate students overall. Some of our best classroom strategies have evolved from trying to figure out how to deal with our more challenging students. When we change our practices, for example, to be more multisensory, project based, and experiential, we are helping the girls tremendously.

In my own school, the so-called "boy-friendly strategies" helped girls attain three times the growth in reading and writing compared to girls in other schools. Boys forced us to address our instructional strategies— and girls benefited along with the boys. Frankly, all kids deserve the best in brain-based, developmentally appropriate, and highly engaging instruction. And if it is boys and their school issues that force us to get to this better place, then so be it!

> Creating a boy-friendly school is not a zero-sum game. It does not come at the expense of girls. My experience has been that creating an environment friendly to boys engages all learners and re-energizes teachers. If we want our children to be eager to come to school and to be engaged in their learning, creating a boy-friendly environment is a crucial step.
>
> Jonathan Wolfer, principal, Douglass Elementary School

SMART Goals

Once you've laid the groundwork with some or all of the activities I've suggested above, you will be ready to develop your school's SMART goal (specific, measurable, attainable, research-based, and time-bound). I won't address this in detail here because this topic is not specific to educating boys and it is addressed thoroughly in other professional resources, including one of my favorites: *Getting Excited About Data: Bringing Together People, Passion and Purpose* (Holcomb, 1999).

One thing that I do suggest keeping in mind is that SMART goals focused on boys' achievement are going to significantly affect your overall school achievement gains since boys are such a large subgroup in a coed school. Also, you will see noticeable gains for your special education subgroup, since approximately 75% of students with special needs are boys. Therefore, if you write an overall school achievement goal for all students and you write a specific school achievement goal (sometimes called an "equity goal") for your subgroup of boys, you have the potential for "wins" on several fronts.

At my former school, when boys made eight times the achievement gains, it pushed our school's growth rating for all students into the highest category, called Significant Improvement. The weight of those boys' scores was enough to swing the entire school's ranking!

DEVELOPING AN ACTION PLAN

I found the following activity to be an effective and organized way to get everyone involved in the brainstorming and selection of intervention strategies for our school improvement plan. I first used this process as a principal in the Boulder Valley School District (when we were writing our school improvement plan to close the gender gap) and have subsequently utilized it numerous times with schools that are looking to operationalize their knowledge and ideas. Faculty will be ready for this conversation once they have some awareness of boy-friendly strategies, even if they still need professional development for implementation.

I suggest giving each group a few copies of these instructions. That way, you can get the groups rolling (i.e., do Step 1 together), and they can work at their own pace through steps 2–5), as opposed to keeping the groups in lockstep together. I provide plenty of time for this activity—depending on the size of your groups, plan on 1.5–2 hours. You will then need time to bring each small group's work back to the large group for further discussion, melding of ideas (eliminating duplicates, etc.), and consensus building around the primary interventions.

DEVELOPING AN ACTION PLAN

Step 1: Define three levels of intervention

Classroom: Intervention strategies at the classroom level are strategies directly related to how and what students are taught. These may vary from class to class based on the needs of students and teachers but are all research based and come from an agreed-upon list developed by the entire faculty.

School: These are intervention strategies that relate to the operation of the school or schoolwide activities. They require everyone's buy-in and support. Examples include things like single-sex classes, advisory periods, vertical mentoring, master scheduling, distribution of resources, professional development, all-school events . . . basically, interventions that, when implemented, affect everyone.

Community: These are intervention strategies that connect the school's work to the community/parents. They require an agreement among faculty members. Community-level strategies might include training for parents, newsletter articles, initiatives to involve dads, business partnerships, social action projects, etc.

Step 2: Give each participant nine index cards or sticky notes. Each participant works alone to brainstorm three strategies for each of the three levels of intervention. *Participants should focus on selecting the strategies that they feel have the greatest chance of increasing student success.* Each strategy is written on a separate card/note.

Step 3: The team now works together to share and explain their strategy ideas. Be specific! The team should eliminate duplicates, blend ideas as appropriate, and then write their combined list of strategies on three separate pieces of flip-chart paper labeled *Classroom*, *School*, and *Community*. Post the charts on the wall and make sure everyone understands what is written.

Step 4: Now, *set aside the Classroom strategies page* and just focus for a moment on the School and Community strategies. Give each participant

(Continued)

(Continued)

six colored dots. Each participant is to affix three dots per page next to the strategies under School and Community that they think would be *most impactful for students.* When this is done, count the colored dots and engage in a discussion about the "top three" group picks. Do these look like good areas of focus for the school and community to engage in this work? Can each member of your team commit to supporting these shared strategies? These strategies will now become part of the school's improvement plan, and everyone is responsible for implementing them.

Step 5: Go back to the Classroom strategies. How many are there? Agree on a number of strategies that each teacher will adopt as his/her professional focus. Consider having each teacher select two or three strategies to implement *that he/she is not already implementing* in the classroom. These strategies can become part of each teacher's professional growth plan, as well as woven into the school improvement plan as Classroom-level strategies.

SCHOOL IMPROVEMENT AND TEACHER GROWTH

Once you have completed the *Developing an Action Plan* activity, you should have a consensus list of seven or eight classroom interventions/strategies. As mentioned in Step 5, it is important to create agreement that all teachers will select two, maybe three, of these strategies to implement in their own classroom. Teachers are asked to select strategies *that they are not currently using* and to serve as a support person for others for the strategies that they do currently use.

These classroom strategies now become part of the teacher's professional goal for the year. If the teacher is on evaluation cycle this year, the strategies and the monitoring of their implementation, along with results, become a part of that process. If the teacher is not on formal evaluation, the process is less formal, but he or she still identifies the strategies, and there are check-in, conferencing, and coaching regarding implementation during the school year.

This has been, in my estimation, the most powerful way to operationalize a school improvement plan. It infuses the overarching school goal into the daily conversations and practices of the school, right down to the level of the classroom. This practice creates intentionality around talking about the school goal and implementation of the school goal in very real ways. For those teachers who are not on evaluation cycle and therefore not bound to specific evaluation timelines, it is helpful to preschedule times for these conversations early on in the school year. Given a weeklong window in early fall, midyear, and end of year, each teacher schedules 20 minutes with you to discuss the strategies, their implementation, any resources needed, and student progress.

This brings us back to the issue of school climate and, more so, school culture. Hopefully, a culture has been established that allows teachers to feel safe to try new things, to be supported when things work *and when they don't work*, and to discuss their students' progress openly without feeling like a meeting with the principal is a "gotcha." One way to accomplish this is to allow teachers to choose how they will present information about their implementation and their students' progress. Some teachers may wish to conference as grade-level teams or departments.

DEVELOPING A YEARLONG PROFESSIONAL DEVELOPMENT PLAN

Let's take a look at the big picture: the yearlong plan for improvement and professional development. I have provided a number of activities that can be organized and scheduled to meet a variety of needs. Some or all of these activities will be done in collaboration with a representative leadership team, and some of the activities will be done as a whole staff. The following list provides an organized recap of what we've discussed previously in this chapter, as well as some new things to consider:

Leader's To-Do List

1. Organize and present data in a visual way. Provide opportunities for stakeholders to discuss the celebrations and challenges they see in the data. Identify the priority challenges to address.

2. Provide opportunities for professional dialogue to explore the knowledge, attitudes, and beliefs held by staff members about boys and boys' education.

3. Develop a SMART goal.

4. Collaboratively develop the school improvement goal interventions with the *Developing an Action Plan* process. Select the strategies and interventions that you, as a team, think will be most effective in improving conditions and opportunities for boys.

5. Have teachers develop their individual professional goals that incorporate classroom strategies from the school improvement goal.

6. Put "conference/coaching weeks" on the school calendar now for early fall, midyear, and end of year. Block out your time these weeks to accommodate one-on-one and grade-level/department meetings with teachers to discuss their professional goals. Have teachers set meeting dates and times during these weeks now.

7. Map out a plan for professional development activities for the year:

   a. Select from the PLC activities suggested above (PLC activities #1–5, and team-building activities), as well as others, and slot them into the schedule now. Give your assistant a list of required materials (copies of articles, flip-chart paper, markers, etc.) for the specific upcoming PLC dates now while you're thinking of it.

   b. Identify other valuable professional readings (see suggestions below) and decide how they can be incorporated into your yearlong plan. For example, will there be required monthly all-staff readings, will the reading be done during staff meeting time as a text-rendering activity, and/or will reading be optional for credit?

c. If you plan to do a book study, get books ordered now to avoid rush shipping costs and to allow some people to get a head start. Now is also a good time to complete any paperwork necessary to receive re-licensure credit.

d. Are there outside learning opportunities for teachers to accelerate their professional development or to take the learning to a deeper level, such as topic-specific online courses, local workshops, blogs, or book studies? Can teachers earn compensation or credit for these?

e. Would you like to bring in an expert on the topic of educating boys for teacher and parent workshops and ongoing consultation? If so, make those contacts immediately to increase your chance of getting your preferred choice of dates and speaker (more on utilizing a professional development consultant later).

f. Make sure that you have a plan for incorporating "brain boosters" and other short team-building activities during every faculty meeting and PLC time. Explain what these activities are now to teachers and have teachers/teams pick dates to be the activity leader.

IN A PRINCIPAL'S WORDS

Every staff meeting and staff development day, teachers share strategies that are making a difference in their classrooms. Anyone struggling with using effective strategies is able to make his or her needs known, and many others come to assist. There is also time to demonstrate how to do certain activities such as brain breaks. Many of our staff meetings consist of our discussing what is working and where we are struggling. Everyone quickly embraced all that was happening and became stronger in their convictions.

Suzie Johnston, former principal, Buffalo Trails Elementary School

(Continued)

(Continued)

I modeled a lot of the brain breaks during our staff retreat. I typed up brain breaks and put these slips of paper in a basket. Every 20–30 minutes, I would randomly ask a teacher to pick a slip and lead the faculty in the brain break. At the day's end, we established our goals for the year and talked about how the brain breaks made us feel as learners. Everyone saw the positive effects of the brain breaks and committed to implementing them into their daily routines.

Trish Greenwood, principal, Telluride Elementary School

The most beneficial practice was to keep it in front of them in little snippets at each staff meeting. It also helped that my key leaders were continuing to provide "what was working for them." For example, a fourth-grade teacher that immediately saw the potential benefit of brain breaks dug into the book and developed "Brain Break Cards" that could be copied on tag board and placed on a ring. She e-mailed these cards to all of the teachers in the building. The teachers, at any time, could then grab the Brain Break Ring and do an activity with their students.

Karie Mize, principal, Pine Tree Elementary School

Recommended Resources

The following resources can be used very effectively, in part or in whole, during professional development times. Consider adding them to your school's professional and parent libraries:

Journal Articles

King, K., & Gurian, M. (2006, September). "Teaching to the Minds of Boys." *Educational Leadership, 64*(1), 56–61.

King, K., Gurian, M., & Stevens, K. (2012, November). "Gender-Friendly Schools." *Educational Leadership, 68*(3), 38–42.

Gurian, M., & Stevens, K. (2004, November). "With Boys and Girls in Mind." *Educational Leadership, (62)*3, 21–26.

Books

Brizendine, L. (2010). *The Male Brain.* New York, NY: Random House.

Cannon, C. (2010). *Winning Back Our Boys: The Ultimate Game Plan for Parents & Teachers.* Scottsdale, AZ: LifeSuccess Publishing.

Center on Education Policy. (2010). *Are There Differences in Achievement Between Boys and Girls?* Washington, DC: Author. Retrieved from http://www.cep-dc.org.

Gurian, M. (2010). *The Purpose of Boys: Helping Our Sons Find Meaning, Significance and Direction in Their Lives.* San Francisco, CA: Jossey-Bass.

Gurian, M., & Stevens, K. (2007). *The Minds of Boys: Saving Our Sons From Falling Behind in Life and School.* San Francisco, CA: Jossey-Bass.

Gurian, M., Stevens, K., & King, K. (2008a). *Strategies for Teaching Boys and Girls: Elementary Level.* San Francisco, CA: Jossey-Bass.

Gurian, M., Stevens, K., & King, K. (2008b). *Strategies for Teaching Boys and Girls: Secondary Level.* San Francisco, CA: Jossey-Bass.

James, A. (2007). *Teaching the Male Brain: How Boys Think, Feel, and Learn in School.* Thousand Oaks, CA: Corwin.

Payne, R., & Slocumb, P. (2011). *Boys in Poverty: A Framework for Understanding Dropout.* Bloomington, IN: Solution Tree Press.

Slocumb, P. (2004). *Hear Our Cry: Boys in Crisis.* Highlands, TX: aha! Process.

Videos

CBS (Director). (2001). *The Delinquents* [Motion Picture]. Available for purchase at: http://gurianinstitute.com/products/products-for-educators.

Thompson, M. (Director). (2006). *Raising Cain* [Motion Picture]. Available for purchase at: http://www.pbs.org/opb/raisingcain.

Internet Resources

Ontario Ministry of Education. (2004). *Me Read? No Way! A Practical Guide to Improving Boys' Literacy Skills.* Retrieved from Ontario Ministry of Education: http://www.edu.gov.on.ca/eng/document/brochure/meread/meread.pdf.

Ontario Ministry of Education. (2009). *Me Read? And How! Ontario Teachers Report on How to Improve Boys' Literacy Skills.* Retrieved from Ontario Ministry of Education: http://www.edu.gov.on.ca/eng/curriculum/meRead_andHow.pdf.

Utilizing a Professional Development Consultant

Many schools choose to enhance their professional development plan with the help of an outside expert in the area of gender differentiation. This brings a level of expertise to your school's work that is not likely to be replicated by an internal staff member. Consultants, unlike teachers or in-house staff developers, are able to devote all of their professional time to reading and writing on a specific topic, such as gender differentiation. Some consultants even have the perspective and knowledge gained from working with educators around the world and in a wide variety of school settings. Their knowledge of current research and their experience with practical application in schools are hard to match.

Ideally, the relationship with the consultant includes components that extend over a period of time. For example, a one-day or multi-day teacher workshop in the fall may be followed by shorter workshops later in the school year, as well as on-site classroom observations, on-site or virtual teacher/team coaching, and online/distance learning opportunities (such as online classes, real-time webinars, and blogs—all facilitated by the consultant). Online classes, in particular, are a great way to get your "new hires" up to speed on your staff's professional development work.

> The change we most need is a change in attitude and approach. Administrators and teachers have to be aware that boys are in trouble in school, that what we have been doing works well for girls and less well for boys. Back in the early '70s, schools became acutely aware that girls were behind in math and science and college admissions. That awareness prompted principals to search for young women science and math teachers, to work on programs that would help girls in math. It worked. Girls closed the gap in math and science. We now need the same effort with boys and writing. New focus, new approaches, not more of the same.
>
> Michael Thompson, PhD, coauthor of *Raising Cain: Protecting the Emotional Life of Boys*, and educational consultant

THE FINAL BUZZER

Creating a boy-friendly school is not a matter of simply creating a list of classroom strategies. It is deeper, more comprehensive work than that. It encompasses a boy's total experience at school, including the school's receptiveness to "boy qualities," as well as the staff and community commitment to launching a focused and sustainable change initiative.

- Real, sustainable school improvement happens in schools with positive school climate and culture. The best interventions get lost, and even blocked, in a school where new ideas cannot flourish. Don't overlook this critical work!

- Help your faculty members explore their knowledge, attitudes, and beliefs about boys. Is there thinking that gets in the way? How can a shared sense of urgency be created?
- Go beyond the "standard data" of test scores to get a more comprehensive picture of how boys are faring in your school. Use your data to tell a compelling story.
- Make your school improvement plan a collaborative affair to get everyone on board with the work. Use the expertise on your staff.
- Don't file your school plan—operationalize it! Some important activities in the planning process will help each staff member understand exactly what his/her role is in helping the school meet its goals.
- Create a yearlong plan for professional development and teacher coaching and support.

Boys don't color within the lines. They run with scissors.

Sandy Lubert, teacher and mother of three boys

 Additional materials and resources related to *Writing the Playbook: A Practitioner's Guide to Creating a Boy-Friendly School* can be found at www.boyfriendlyschools.com. Kelley King can be reached at kelleykingpd@hotmail.com.

Leveling the Playing Field

School Policies and Procedures That Don't Squeeze Boys Out

We need to look at school from boys' point of view.
What is working for them, and what is not?

Ralph Fletcher, author of *Guy-Write:*
What Every Guy Writer Needs to Know
and *Boy Writers: Reclaiming Their Voices*

How often do we make time to truly and deeply consider the experience of a boy in our school? What is it like for him to come to this indoor place every day where he works quietly, collaboratively, cooperatively on predominately verbal tasks in artificial lighting? To a place where he does fine-motor tasks, isn't allowed to run with big sticks, and must remember to staple the rough draft to the back of the final draft—or risk losing points? What is it like for him to come to a place where he is taught things without any sense of how these things will help him do something really important in life—like ride a skateboard or perfect his baseball swing? To a place where you get in trouble for doing really cool stuff, like farting, head-locking, and jumping from high places?

This very provocative *New York Times* Letter to the Editor was written by Dr. Nelson Horseman (2006), professor of Molecular and Cellular Physiology at the University of Cincinnati—obviously, an accomplished male learner! He challenges us to think differently, much as Ralph Fletcher does:

To the Editor:

David Brooks ("The Gender Gap at School," column, June 11) addresses important issues about why boys are falling behind in schools. The scale of the challenge goes far beyond reading lists that fail to appeal to boys.

To see the problem clearly, imagine being a girl in a school that is the mirror image of today's schools.

Imagine a school where the vast majority of teachers and administrators are men and where competitive sports are compulsory.

Imagine that students get rewarded for being overly aggressive in school and that there is a zero tolerance policy for being passive.

Imagine getting extra credit for resisting authority, and having points deducted for being compliant with arbitrary rules and meaningless deadlines.

A school like this would feel as hostile to girls as today's schools feel to boys.

As parents generally know, and schools generally ignore, boys and girls need different kinds of experiences and training as they grow. Book lists that appeal are part of the answer, but not all of it.

Dr. Nelson D. Horseman
Professor, University of Cincinnati

We must examine more than just what happens in the classroom if we want to transform the school. We need policies that draw boys in, not push them out; that channel their energy, not squelch it; that hold them accountable, not let them off the hook. And we need everyone on the same page, including teachers, administrators, secretaries, teacher assistants, custodians, bus drivers, parents—everyone who comes in contact with our students.

TRY THIS

Ask your staff to put on a "boy lens," read through your school's student handbook, and have a conversation about what might not be working well for boys. A surprising amount of "gender bias" can be found in school rules. If you find that this is a provocative conversation for your staff, then great! That makes it all the more worthwhile.

EXPECTATIONS AND THE STEREOTYPE THREAT

While the stereotype threat is not something you'll find addressed in a school handbook, it exists, unintentionally, in the subculture of many schools. It has a very definite effect on student outcomes and definitely deserves a thoughtful conversation with faculty and staff. Research demonstrates that the very existence of a negative stereotype such as "Boys are better than girls in math" or "Girls are better behaved than boys" suppresses the test performance of members of the negatively stereotyped group. Therefore,

> There are rules and regulations that are clearly anti-male in many areas. This can be exemplified by how often words such as "harassment," "physical abuse," and "verbal assault" are used to describe teenage boys' behavior. Clearly, boys need consequences for misbehavior, but our perceptions of boys and the very vocabulary we use is skewed to the point that it implies criminal intent where none exists.
>
> Adam Fels, principal, Louisville Middle School

it is absolutely critical that, during the course of addressing gender gaps at your school, negative stereotypes are not created or perpetuated.

The research in this area is compelling and crosses gender and race lines. Females, who are being tested in math and are told that males score better, will perform worse than females who are not told that males do better. Perhaps even more surprisingly, females perform less well when taking math tests alongside boys, when they are given a math test by a male instructor, and when they are required to indicate their sex on the form at the beginning of the test. Even passing reminders that someone belongs to a stereotyped group hurts test performance (APA, 2006). African Americans have shown similar results when told that white students perform better and when they have to mark their ethnicity on the test. In one study (Ciani & Sheldon, 2010), students were told to write the letter "A," "J" or "F" at the top of their test sheet. Those who marked an "A" on their test scored better than both the "J" (neutral) and the "F" (negative) groups.

This brings us to a rather interesting study, *Gender Expectations and Stereotype Threat* (Hartley & Sutton, 2010), which argues that lower expectations of boys is contributing to widening gender gaps. Girls' performance, on the other hand, is boosted by what they perceive to be their teachers' belief that they will do better in school and be better behaved. Even the children themselves develop opinions about which gender does better in school. The study's author, Bonnie Hartley, states, "By seven or eight years old, children of both genders believe that boys are less focused, able and successful than girls—and think that adults endorse this stereotype. There are signs that these expectations have the potential to become self-fulfilling in influencing children's actual conduct and achievement."

DISCIPLINE

Suspension

By eighth grade, nearly one boy in four has been suspended for at least one day, while only one out of 10 girls had been, according to Marianne Bertrand and Jessica Pan in their study, *The Trouble With Boys: Social Influences and the Gender Gap in Disruptive Behavior* (2011). These findings are based on American students who were tracked from kindergarten through 12th grade. And it doesn't end there—the gender gap has worsened over time. During the period from 1980 to 2006, suspension rates for boys went from nearly 16% to 24%. Girls' rates stayed flat over the same period. Between 1993 and 2003, suspensions doubled in the Chicago public schools to top 20,000.

> The zero-tolerance policies that schools adopted after Columbine have been almost completely ineffective in changing boys' behavior, but such rules have resulted in more boys being suspended . . . and suspended again, and ultimately expelled. Rigid by-the-book discipline often overpunishes boys, and research shows that it does not work. Only meaningful relationships and clear consequences from adults whom boys respect actually work.
>
> Michael Thompson, PhD, coauthor of *Raising Cain: Protecting the Emotional Lives of Boys*

There is no research to support that suspensions serve as a deterrent to misbehavior. In fact, the research identifies strong correlations between suspensions and dropping out of school. Students who are suspended one time during their K–12 education are 16% less likely to go to college. Part of this is because suspensions result in a loss of instructional time and serve to disenfranchise the very students who can least afford to be kept out of the classroom. Further exacerbating the problems with suspension is the fact that black and Hispanic youth are suspended at a much higher rate for the same infractions as their white peers.

> What are we teaching our boys if, when they misbehave, they get a free ticket home? Are we in fact honoring their wishes to disconnect from school? We need to focus on a problem-solving process that becomes a teaching process.
>
> Jonathan Wolfer, principal, Douglass Elementary School

A major responsibility of any administrator is to ensure the safety and well-being of all students and staff. Of course, there are circumstances in which the removal of a student from the school property is necessary—but these situations are far fewer than current suspension rates indicate. When off-campus suspension is absolutely necessary, some school districts provide an alternative to staying home. Students report to an alternate site where they receive access to academics, time to discuss their infraction, counseling, and community service work.

> **Goals of Restorative Justice**
>
> - Hold the offender accountable for his or her actions
> - Provide victims with a safe place to share how the incident impacted him or her
> - Include members of the community in developing a moral stance and helping the offender in making things right
> - Develop an effective alternative to the traditional system of school discipline
>
> Source: From Restorative Solutions, available at: http://www.restorativesolutions.us/schools.html

In most cases of misconduct, there is a better solution: Keep boys in school (perhaps in an alternate location). Students stay connected to their academics and don't get a "day off," which, for many students, means a day of unsupervised "who-knows-what." Have the student develop and carry out a plan to repair the harm that he has caused to his community. This is embodied in a program called Restorative Discipline—a program developed for schools based on the criminal justice system's Restorative Justice. Through a Restorative Discipline approach, students receive the guidance and support that they need for becoming more empathetic and changing their conduct, while receiving the message: "We care about you and are invested in you being successful here."

TRY THIS

Many emotionally charged situations with students can be de-escalated with the right strategies:

- Don't chastise a young man in front of his peers. It may cause resentment and seriously compromise your relationship going forward. Talk to him in private (Kindlon & Thompson, 1999).
- Give angry or upset students some water to drink. Within minutes of drinking water, the primary stress chemical in the blood (cortisone) starts to drop (Batmanghelidi, 1997).
- Give the student some time and space to regroup. If the boy is not ready to talk, give him some space and don't push it. "Cooling off" is a powerful method for shifting from anger to calmness (Goleman, 2006). Go check your e-mail or find some other excuse to allow the boy some alone time.
- Go for a walk. The physical movement further reduces stress levels while increasing blood flow and oxygen to the brain (American College of Sports Medicine, 2010).
- Don't insist on eye contact. This can create an unnecessary power struggle especially with an angry boy. Oftentimes, lack of eye contact is indicative of a feeling of insecurity, not disrespect. Going for a walk while you talk allows you to naturally converse shoulder-to-shoulder without necessitating eye contact (Roberts, 2001).

IN A PRINCIPAL'S WORDS

As an administrator, I have been repeatedly surprised at how well my disciplinary meetings go when I allow boys time to sit and cool down before we speak. I often bring them into my office and go and check a few e-mails before I ask them what happened on the playground or in the classroom. These small steps help to diminish hot-headed behaviors and get kids back in the classroom where they should be.

Trish Greenwood, principal, Telluride Elementary School

(Continued)

(Continued)

When boys are struggling to engage in a lesson and other strategies are not helping, we go for "walkabouts." These consist of going outside, running back and forth, and getting the fidgets out. Then we talk about what was hindering them in the classroom.

Desha Bierbaum, principal, Wamsley Elementary School

Walking and talking is a strategy I use with boys in a disciplinary setting. In a tense situation, I will not speak to the boy until they can calmly answer arbitrary questions. Things only escalate when you demand they look at you and answer questions immediately. Quite honestly, sometimes I can't speak or answer when angry, so no wonder it is hard for them!

Jim Weber, vice principal, Mount Carmel High School

Taking Away Recess as Punishment

"It's a big mistake for a teacher to punish a child for bad behavior by denying recess," asserts Dr. Romina Barros, a pediatrician and assistant professor at Albert Einstein College of Medicine. Her 2009 study followed 11,000 third-graders and found that students' classroom behavior (as ranked by classroom teachers) was significantly better for students receiving at least 15 minutes of recess per day. Dr. Barros adds, "Recess should be part of the curriculum. You don't punish a kid by having them miss math class, so kids shouldn't be punished by not getting recess" (Barros, Silver, & Stein, 2009). Dr. Joseph Tobin, professor at Arizona State University, states "Eliminating recess only heightens boys' active and aggressive impulses. The very boys who tend to be punished are the ones who most need physical release from their tension. If we take away their only opportunity to deal with that stress, they may become more tense and then find it even more difficult to sit still and focus on their schoolwork" (PBS Parents, n.d.b, ¶ 2).

In response to the over-whelming and conclusive research on the importance of recess for all students (and especially boys!), some school districts are modifying their district wellness policies. In 2009, Hopkinton Public Schools in Mass-achusetts revised its district policy to request that teach-ers limit the use of recess as a time to administer disci-pline or have students make up work. Similarly, the New York City Department of Education wellness policy discourages school personnel from withholding physical activity (recess or physical education) from students as a form of punishment.

> Time out for behavior infractions is likely one of the greatest ways to cause boys difficulties. To address this, we did away with "sitting on the line" at recess and created a "walking" time out. The students, both boys and girls, now walk back and forth along the sidewalk for their time out rather than sitting.
>
> Desha Bierbaum, principal, Wamsley Elementary School

Consider these alternatives to withholding recess as punishment:

- Confine the student to a certain area of the playground for a day or week;
- Restrict access to playing a certain game(s) for a day or week;
- Restrict certain children from playing together for a set period of time;
- Have the student walk laps around the track or around the school yard during recess instead of sitting against the wall; or
- Take away a student's in-class "free choice" time instead of taking away recess.

In cases where you do not want a student on the playground at all, find a physical task for the student that helps out around the school rather than having the student sit in the classroom or detention. One inventive principal in Rifle, Colorado, had students help sand wooden stools that a parent had made for classrooms. Other principals have had students help wipe tables in the cafeteria, pick up trash, or sweep pea gravel instead of making them sit through their recess, only to return to class with a lot of unspent energy!

TRY THIS

Gather all staff (including recess supervisors) together to introduce current research on recess and the issues of withholding recess as a form of discipline. Examine recent changes in wellness policies governing recess in some districts. Have staff members engage in small-group conversations and document their discussion:

- What are the most common offenses that result in loss of recess/break at our school?
- Who is most often losing recess/break? (i.e., by gender, grade level)
- What alternatives exist for withholding recess/break at our school?
- What is an alternative to making students sit during a lost recess?

Corporal Punishment/"Paddling"

Corporal punishment in schools, while on the decline, remains legal in 19 U.S. states and is used frequently in 13—Missouri, Kentucky, Texas, Oklahoma, Arkansas, Louisiana, Mississippi, Alabama, Georgia, South Carolina, North Carolina, Tennessee, and Florida—according to 2008 data from the Office for Civil Rights at the U.S. Department of Education (Institute of Education Sciences, 2008). More than 100 countries worldwide have banned paddling in schools, including all of Europe and Canada.

The use of corporal punishment is not supported in research and, in fact, is almost overwhelmingly associated with negative effects. "It increases children's problem behavior over time," states Elizabeth Gershoff, a University of Michigan assistant professor of social work. "Children learn to solve problems using aggression, and a sense of resentment can cause them to act out more" (Gershoff, 2002). If corporal punishment is still used in your school, it is time to look for alternative means of disciplining students that are less discriminatory, less fear based, and less likely to cause resentment, and that focus on developing problem-solving skills and self-control.

Quick Stats on Paddling

- In states where paddling is most common, black girls are paddled more than twice as often as white girls.
- African American students in general are 1.4 times more likely to be paddled.
- Boys are three times as likely to be paddled as girls.
- Special education kids are more likely to be paddled than nondisabled students.

Source: U.S. Department of Education, 2007.

Cell Phones and Discipline

Cell phones, once considered a distraction, are becoming increasingly accepted on school campuses. As schools spend more and more time disciplining students who violate cell phone policies, and with the inevitable growth in the use of personal devices, times are indeed changing. The Chinese say, "It's easier to ride a horse in the direction it's already going." Look—we know that handheld devices are not going away. And we've got a highly motivating, highly engaging piece of technology here that's in the hands of expert users. There is a huge opportunity here!

Frankly, given how cell phones are akin to a person's right arm nowadays, I cannot imagine any adult being able to comply with policies that completely restrict access to their cell phones for seven straight hours. Ultimately, these highly restrictive policies don't eliminate student cell phone use; rather, the policies just push it underground, and students get sneaky. As the use of personal technology and capability only continues to expand, schools with bans will spend more and more time enforcing a rule that will eventually go the way of the dinosaur.

Here are a few examples of current cell phone policies at schools. Where does your school fall? Is your policy enforceable?

- Cell phone ban: Students are not permitted to have a cell phone in their possession on school grounds for any reason.
- Cell phone check-in: Students may bring a phone onto campus, but they must check it in at the beginning of the day and check it out at the end of the day.
- Cell phones can be on campus but not visible during school hours: Students may carry a cell phone, but they must be turned off and out of sight the entire school day, including on student breaks such as lunch time.
- Cell phone as educational tool: Students are permitted to bring their cell phone to school, and cell phones are used as a learning tool in the classroom. Students receive training in proper cell phone etiquette at the beginning of the school year. Students may use cell phones for personal use during transitions and lunch. Students must have cell phones turned off when entering a classroom.

Interestingly, we can look to the U.S. Department of Education's *National Education Technology Plan* (2010) for direction on this topic. The Plan supports cell phone use, stating that districts are finding that student use of personal digital devices can be beneficial and safe when staff training is provided and ground rules are set. Examples of their recommended ground rules include:

- Cell phone use is allowed only for working on assignments;
- Text and video can be sent only with a teacher's permission;
- No photographing, or video or audio recording is allowed; and,
- No posting of content to a website is allowed without permission.

So how does this relate to our conversation about boys in school? Well, perhaps there is less of a gender distinction here, but one of the big things we need to think about when working with boys is "pick your battles!" More rules aren't necessarily better . . . and I would argue that, for boys especially, it is definitely not better. Boys already have lots of ways to run afoul of school—be cautious of creating one more way. Ideally, schools will move to a place where personal digital devices are embraced as educational tools. For all students—and for boys in particular—we need to find ways to bring the real world into the learning experience.

TIME, PLACE, AND MANNER

Boys bump up against the boundaries regularly, and, most of the time, it's an issue of what I call "Time, Place, and Manner." For example, roughhousing with a friend in the backyard is okay, but not in the school hallway. Relieving oneself against a tree is okay on a camping trip, but not on the school playground. Instead of telling the boy that he is bad or that his behavior is bad, make it clear that there is a better *time, place,* or *manner* for the behavior. Help him identify when and where certain behaviors are okay and when they are not.

SCHOOLS PUTTING IT INTO ACTION

At our school we have designated playground areas that are for walk and talk, and other areas for running and throwing balls. On snow days we have created snowball targets to give the students a safe environment to throw snow.

Grade 8 teacher of an all-boys' class

Our boys were always climbing up the slide as children were trying to slide down. We decided to make Fridays "opposite day." On that day each week, the rule is that you can only go up the slide. We no longer need to be constantly reprimanding the boys.

Desha Bierbaum, principal, Wamsley Elementary School

(Continued)

(Continued)

Do we penalize and discipline our boys for boy-typical behavior—such as roughhousing and physical play? Or do we use these experiences as teachable moments—teaching boys what is appropriate behavior at certain times of the day?

Jonathan Wolfer, principal, Douglass Elementary School

I remember boys getting sent to my office for fighting. "No," I'd say, "actually they are just getting to know each other." We need to understand the difference. Intent is important and, so often with boys, intent is misread.

Vermelle Greene, principal/founder (retired), SACRED Life Boys Academy

GRADES AND HOMEWORK

I think it is too bad that by sixth grade you get loaded down with homework. Too much of it is useless in everyday life.

Jacob, age 13

Boys earn 70% of the *D*s and *F*s and less than 50% of the *A*s. Almost 50% of girls have a 3.0 grade point average or better. Only 33% of boys do. The gender gap in grade point average boils down to behavior: Boys are far more likely to turn in homework late, or not at all. "Basically what schools are doing is grading behavior that is not based on what students know," states Julie Coates, coauthor of *Smart Boys, Bad Grades: Why Boys Get Worse Grades and Are Only 35% of Graduates in Higher Education.* "As long as grades include academic assignments of grades for nonacademic behavior, boys will be on the short end" (Draves & Coates, 2006). Michael Thompson, coauthor of *Raising Cain: Protecting the Emotional Life of Boys,* says that "girls are the gold standard for being a student. What does that mean for boys—that they are defective girls?" For Dr. Thompson it comes down to this: Girls "do school" better than boys (Tyre, 2006).

Teachers often argue that homework teaches responsibility and prepares students for the workplace. In their provocative report, *Smart Boys, Bad Grades,* Bill Draves and Julie Coates turn this logic on its head. Gender differences related to late or missing work have been documented only in academia, not in the workplace. "Homework offenders" during the school years do not turn into irresponsible employees in the workplace (Draves & Coates, 2006).

Let Grades Reflect Mastery

The standards-based grading movement is good for boys because it puts more emphasis on mastery than on compliance. At most, 10% of a grade is made up of Practice and Preparation (homework completion) and the remaining 90% of the grade to formative and summative assessments and assignments. Other schools have instituted polices that homework does not count toward a student's grade, but the student cannot retake tests for better scores unless they have completed the homework. This can be a fair way to respond to critics who would say that standards-based grading allows students to slack off on homework.

TRY THIS

Download and make copies of "Smart Boys, Bad Grades" (http://www.smartboysbadgrades.com/smartboys_badgrades.pdf). Use this article to initiate a conversation about homework at your school:

- What issues does the article raise?
- Do classroom practices vary in terms of handling late work?
- What policies and practices can we adopt that are more "boy friendly" and that will make grades more a reflection of mastery rather than behavior?

For more ideas about grading practices, check out Ken O'Connor's "15 Fixes for Broken Grades" in his book *A Repair Kit for Grading: Fifteen Fixes for Broken Grades* (2010).

"Good" Homework for Boys

Make a schoolwide commitment to ban busy work and make homework as relevant as possible. For example, have students conduct interviews, make models, conduct Internet research, or go on "scavenger hunts." For older students, have them create (on chart paper) a Facebook page for a historical character, including status updates, friends, and "likes," or create a Twitter account, complete with followers, top tweets, and hashtags. Students can create a book trailer (similar to a movie trailer) as a book report and post it to YouTube. Andrew, an eighth-grade student, says that homework should be "as hands-on as possible. Students have spent long days in class already. With homework, let kids do something other than more sitting." Sometimes, plain ol' skill practice is necessary; however, I have seen math teachers

> Homework puts kids into two categories: smart and dumb.
>
> 14-year-old boy

What do boys have to say about homework? Here is a sampling of their responses

I don't like homework that:

- is long and tedious and is just something you already know too well and is just a countless amount of time-consuming practice. —Erik, eighth-grader
- goes past the point of learning and you are trying just to do pointless busy work.—Alex, ninth-grader
- is repetitive and doesn't stimulate the brain. If the brain isn't stimulated, then the students will have a lack of interest at school.—Roman, sixth-grader
- just takes up time and doesn't make you think.—Joe, eighth-grader
- has large numbers of tedious problems which require no thought. Adam, 10th-grader

assign 90–100 math problems a night. Needless, to say, there has got to be a balance. Let's find a way to take the "kill" out of "drill."

BANNING AGGRESSION THEMES

There is no such thing as violent play. Violence and aggression are intended to hurt somebody. Play is not intended to hurt somebody. Play, rougher in its themes and rougher physically, is a feature of boyhood in every society on Earth.

Michael Thompson, coauthor of *Raising Cain: Protecting the Emotional Lives of Boys*

The fantasy lives of boys are filled with themes of aggression and conflict, as well as all things gross—farts, barf, blood, guts, you name it! And who appreciates these topics more than another boy in class? As *Guy-Write* and *Boy Writers* author Ralph Fletcher (2012), points out: "Boys write for boys." No truer words were ever spoken! While girls generally gravitate to relational themes revolving around friends and family (as well as fanciful creatures such as fairies, unicorns, and mermaids at younger ages), boys go for action and edginess. Whether it is going for the laugh or grossing people out that fires that boy up, there is amazing motivation for learning if we harness it in the right way. In fact, testing the boundaries of so-called "school appropriateness" can

> Many teachers find boys' interests in violence, gross things, and bodily functions to be boring or stupid. We need to recognize that many of us have internal prejudices against these interests. Just as we used to ask ourselves in the '70s, "In what ways am I being sexist in my treatment of girls?" we now have to ask, "In what ways are we disapproving of boys' interests in our classrooms?"
>
> Joseph Tobin, PhD, professor, Arizona State University, author of *Good Guys Don't Wear Hats*

actually turn a so-called reluctant reader into a voracious one; a reluctant writer into a prolific one.

So what are appropriate topics for school? This question has as many answers as there are teachers. When I talk to teachers about this, their answers range from "I don't allow any guns in stories" to "There can't be blood in stories" to "I don't set limits except for obviously bad things like naming someone in class who gets hurt." It also depends on the age of students involved. Female teachers, generally speaking, are more conservative in their thinking than male teachers. Secondary teachers tend to worry that violent writing could foretell violent behavior. Primary teachers tend to worry more about upsetting young classmates, oftentimes the girls. In all cases, we need to stop and think about the audience. Who will read this piece? Is it a private piece in a student journal? Or does the student want to publish it in the school newspaper? The answers to these questions can go a long way toward determining what boundaries to set, and when.

> One third-grade boy sharing his story idea with another boy: "So there's this dog and he poops and barfs at the same time! And then he does it again and the poop is even *bigger* this time!"

TRY THIS

Here are some steps to stimulating a meaningful conversation on the issue of aggression themes in writing at the elementary level:

- Show the clip called "Seth" from the PBS video, *Raising Cain* (available at www.pbs.org):
- Have teachers debrief the video in small groups:
  o What are the implications for our practice?
  o What kinds of limits do we put on the expression of aggression and why?
  o Are any of these limitations squelching boys' desire to write?
  o How does the principle of "Time, Place, and Manner" (see earlier in this chapter) relate to the issue of boys' topic choice in writing?

- Ask teachers to collect samples of student writing with strong aggression themes over the next month. Look for pieces that push the envelope. Set a meeting date in the future for them to bring the samples back to the group.
- Share and discuss the student writing samples:
  o Is this writing "out of bounds" for anyone? If so, why or why not?
  o What background information about the writing piece or about the student might be helpful in gaining a better perspective on the nature of the aggression here?
  o How has teacher thinking about this issue evolved through the course of this discussion?
  o What are appropriate steps/interventions when a teacher feels unsure/uncomfortable with a piece of writing and how to respond to it?
- Discuss as a whole group how classrooms can adopt a balanced approach to addressing normal aggression themes that manifest themselves in writing—an approach that doesn't squelch boys while ensuring a safe and respectful environment for everyone.

THE FINAL BUZZER

In this chapter, we dealt with some very common and well-intended school practices that have unintended outcomes for boys. This chapter can provide a launching point for schoolwide discussions with staff, students, and the broader community.

> For many boys the act of writing is a painful experience in many ways: both physically and emotionally. There is nothing worse than to create a great story full of action, intrigue, explosions, and gore only to have a teacher suggest the writing should be edited of all violence.
>
> Eighth-grade all-boys classroom teacher

- Many school policies, practices, and procedures are established with the best of intentions, but without carefully considering how they affect boys.

- The "stereotype threat" is an often invisible yet powerful presence in school organizations. Research shows that it is growing the gender gap in schools.
- Some common forms of school discipline are very unproductive for boys, and even counterproductive! It's important to evaluate your school's discipline plan with boys in mind.
- Are you trying to enforce outdated cell phone policies and wonder if you are losing the battle? It is time to get these tantalizing devices working *for* us, not against us.
- Many discipline problems can be defused, or avoided incompletely, with the use of a boy-friendly approach.
- Teach students about "Time, Place, & Manner"—many typical boy behaviors are fine in some situations but not in others. Help boys learn the difference.
- Homework issues, not lack of mastery, is the number one reason for boys' lower grades. Reevaluate your homework and grading policies if student grades are more about compliance than about mastery.
- Aggression themes figure prominently in boys' fantasy lives and sometimes make the adults uncomfortable; however, arbitrary "no blood" rules in classrooms shut boys down.

Create an environment where boyhood is celebrated.

Brewster Ely, headmaster, Town School for Boys

 Additional materials and resources related to *Writing the Playbook: A Practitioner's Guide to Creating a Boy-Friendly School* can be found at www.boyfriendlyschools.com. Kelley King can be reached at kelleykingpd@hotmail.com.

5

Touching Base

Relationship Building to Guide Boys on Their Journey

If you want the boys to jump through hoops for you, you better be prepared to be there for them . . . it's all about respect.

Eighth-grade teacher of an all-boys classroom

It's 7 o'clock in the morning, and my son and I walk into the geometry teacher's classroom. It is our prearranged meeting to discuss how my son might improve his grades. He has too many zeroes in the grade book. We take our seats in two student desks and wait for the teacher to join us. After rummaging through her briefcase, the teacher walks over, slaps some papers on the desk in front of my son and says, "Why don't we start by having you explain why you chose to doodle on this math packet instead of getting it done?" My heart sinks. I know where this is going. I look over at my son, and I see his eyeballs literally recede into their sockets. He glazes over, pulls back. He disengages. I feel a lump form in my throat. This meeting was supposed to help make things better, but I can already see that that won't happen.

The teacher, on the other hand, seems unaware of the monumental shift that just occurred. She continues to stand. In fact, she stands for the entire 20 minutes—standing over us, looking down on us, as we look up at her.

I have learned through my son, and through my work as an educator, that a boy can love or hate a class based on his relationship with the teacher. One year he can love Spanish, next year he can hate it. One year he can earn a high *B* in math, another year he barely scrapes by with a low *C*. I really wish it wasn't so—I want my son to consistently do his best, regardless! I implore: "Your grade shouldn't depend on whether or not you like the teacher!," and "The teacher doesn't get the grade—you do!" And so the conversation goes.

While the teacher-student relationship dynamic is true for many boys (and most certainly for the ones you are thinking about as you read this book), it's not this way for every boy. Some boys do well regardless of the teacher. These are the boys who are good at "doing school." They know how the system works, they conform to the system, they tend not to question it (even if they don't like it), and they have the skills to be successful: *They like school, and school likes them.* But for the boy who struggles in school or feels disconnected from school for any reason, his relationship with the teacher is a critical element in whether or not he is going to be successful.

Part of this is biologically based, as discussed in Chapter 2. From the earliest of ages, little boys have less of the "people pleaser" hormone, called oxytocin, and are therefore more likely to get restless and to question the relevancy of schoolwork. Boys are less chemically driven to work hard to please the teacher, as compared to girls. But that oxytocin level is not a static thing. Being in the presence of someone who likes us does, in and of itself, increase our oxytocin levels. If a boy feels liked and valued, he'll run through a wall for a teacher. If he doesn't feel liked, however, he can easily check out—or worse. This trend shows up early for some boys and becomes more prevalent among boys as they enter adolescence—a time when societal and peer pressures become stronger.

Understanding the biological underpinnings of being male in a society with very clear definitions of what masculinity is (and is not) is critical to knowing how we can set the stage for success. For some boys, many factors conspire against them, including being strongly "male brained" in a traditional classroom setting, receiving societal messages that it is not cool to be a good student, and having a lack of male role models and home support. Some students face extraordinary social issues, such as poverty, family stress, unemployment, and fatherlessness. These conditions inhibit the child's brain development (E. Jensen, 2009), as well as the formation of healthy social relationships. Many of these highly impacted young people seek out gangs to fill their need for acceptance and direction on their journey to manhood (Cannon, 2010). For all boys and young men—and especially those who are disadvantaged—the relationships that a boy forms at school *become the single most important variable* in determining the child's ability to rise above circumstances.

WHAT BOYS HAVE TO SAY

Not liking my teacher ruined a lot of fifth grade for me. I couldn't get around it and got into a lot of trouble.

Jacob, age 13

You have to like a teacher in order to want to do their work.

Rick, age 15

I don't want to impress a teacher that I don't like. I don't care about making them proud.

Jared, age 12

There is an emotional tension that exists between me and a teacher that I don't like. It can start a fire very easily.

Jihoon, age 17

(Continued)

(Continued)

They don't respect me so why should I respect them?
Greg, age 17

Not having a good relationship with a teacher turns off my desire to learn.
Joe, age 16

When I don't respect the teacher, I refuse to learn from him or her.
Adam, age 16

A bad relationship with my teacher affects my attitude. I just screw off and listen to my iPod and stuff.
James, age 14

I usually never talk to a teacher I don't like if I don't have to. And if I fail the class? Oh well.
Joey, age 16

THE SOCIAL-EMOTIONAL LIVES OF BOYS

From a very young age, children begin to develop their self-identity relative to those around them. Any kindergarten teacher, for example, will tell you that the "mean girl" behavior has already started. Children start to see themselves and others in groups—"the smart kids," "the dumb kids," "the class clown," "the jocks," and so on. In terms of academic ability, children are very observant about things like the color (level) of the spelling book they are in and who is in the highest reading group and who is in the lowest group. There are some interesting gender differences when it comes to how boys and girls perceive and internalize these realities and how it transfers into their social-emotional well-being at school.

Emotional literacy

According to psychotherapist Claude Steiner (2003), emotional literacy is "the ability to understand one's own feelings and those of others in order to facilitate relationships." With all of the social, emotional, and academic challenges of the typical school day, emotional literacy is an important ingredient for success; however, boys lag behind girls in this area. Studies on gender differences in emotional intelligence indicate that socialization and societal stereotypes are the most significant contributors to the variations in emotional literacy between males and females. Based on studies by King (1999); Sutarso (1999); Ryff, Singer, Wing, and Love (2001); and Singh (2002), females are, on average, more aware of their emotions, more empathetic, and more adept interpersonally. Females are also able to more accurately identify the emotions of others by viewing facial expressions. Sixteen-year-old Austin's comment illustrates the dichotomy in teen-think: "I'm not an adolescent. I take control of my own emotions."

> Many boys are rough and tough on the outside, but they all want to succeed, feel appreciated and valued, and be understood.
>
> Betsy Hoke, retired elementary school principal

Another component of emotional literacy is self-regulation. Again, this is an area of greater challenge, in general, for boys compared to girls. The center of self-regulation in the brain is the prefrontal cortex. This area is like the "police officer" of the brain. It helps to mediate strong emotions, reduce impulsivity, and delay gratification. Because the frontal lobes develop later in boys (James, 2007), boys are slower to develop the skills of self-regulation. Additionally, less connectivity between the emotional centers of the brain and the verbal processing regions mean boys frequently have greater difficulty putting words to their feelings (Lee & Owens, 2003). This can inhibit the development of self-awareness, problem solving, and verbal conflict mediation.

In high-poverty environments, the development of emotional literacy skills is further impacted due to the lack of reliable caregivers, predictable home environments, and modeling of healthy behavior. This can lead to social and emotional dysfunction for students, such as giving up on school tasks or having difficulty working cooperatively with groups. Lack of emotional regulation, as well as a lack of an adequate emotional vocabulary, can cause teachers to interpret students' behavior as disrespectful when, in fact, these students have a smaller repertoire of social and emotional skill sets to draw upon (Jensen, 2009). Being a male-brained boy living in poverty can be a bit of a double whammy. These boys require a special level of understanding and support to develop the emotional literacy skills that are so crucial to their success.

The Notion of Masculinity

"Masculine"—

1. Having qualities traditionally ascribed to men, as strength and boldness.

2. Possessing characteristics typical of or appropriate to a man; manly.

"Macho"—

1. Having or characterized by qualities considered manly, especially when manifested in an assertive, self-conscious, or dominating way.

2. Having a strong or exaggerated sense of power or the right to dominate.

Source: www.dictionary.com

These definitions are a wonderful jumping-off point for a discussion with boys and young men. These are the times that a single-sex classroom, or at least a single-sex advisory period, is invaluable. How many boys have really considered the difference between being "masculine" and being "macho?"

Do boys err on the side of being macho in their misinformed or unrefined quest for masculinity? What is more noble—being masculine or being macho? We can be guides on a boy's path from boyhood to manhood—to be, as Michael Gurian calls it in *A Fine Young Man: What Parents, Mentors, and Educators Can Do to Shape Adolescent Boys Into Exceptional Men,* "a refiner of the boy's fire." If we, as parents and educators, do not create opportunities for this kind of self-exploration, from where will the boy draw his concept of what it is to be male? From the television or the movies? From video games? From the sports world? From gangs?

> Boys desire a sense of direction; they desire to define a "purpose" for themselves. But they can't do it on their own. Your boys may whine about the demands placed on them, but, in their heart, they have a thirst for the right direction. When I took on the role of educator, I took on a vocation that goes beyond the classroom walls. It is my responsibility to help these boys during their journey to manhood. For young men, it is not always about a specific destination; it is about the quest. And on their quest, they need heroes. They are the lighthouse, and I must meet them where they are.
>
> Frank Lazarek, assistant principal of faculty, O'Dea High School

Mask of Masculinity

Young males often adopt a tough guy persona that can manifest itself in the form of fist bumps, friendly dissing, and swearing, to aggressive confrontations and fighting. Michael Thompson calls this tough, posturing exterior the "mask of masculinity." To adults, this "Don't mess with me" front can be interpreted as angry and distant, and can make teachers (especially female teachers) hesitant or even fearful to reach out to the boy. "The kind of man so many poor boys want to be is a mythical tough guy," says Geoffrey Canada, president of the Harlem Children's Zone. "Boys want to emulate this behavior. It leads to boys posturing themselves in a way that says to the world, 'I am not afraid.'"

In reality, as Dan Kindlon and Michael Thompson (1999) tell us in *Raising Cain,* these boys are concealing a much more complex inner emotional life than they want us to know. Sadness and fear are often behind some of the angriest demeanors. When we, as adults, can see past this mask of masculinity and see the hurting little boy on the inside, our response to that little boy or young man will be much different—we reach out toward that boy, instead of pulling away.

TRY THIS

- Have faculty members view the segment titled "Hugo" from Michael Thompson's video, *Raising Cain* (2006). This video clip can be effective with community groups as well. This clip gives an inside look at the lives of inner-city teen boys living in poverty.
- Optional: Access the video's discussion guide at http://www.pbs .org/opb/raisingcain/discussionguides.html
- Create discussion prompts that personalize the issues presented in the video, such as:

  o What are the implications of this information for us?
  o What are the important takeaways in this video, and what do we need to know and be able to do in order to better support our boys?
  o In what ways do we see the mask of masculinity manifested in our boys?
  o How might we educate our community regarding these issues?

- Provide an opportunity for small-group discussion and whole-group sharing.
- Agree on any follow-up needed and establish timelines.

Pecking Order

An additional social-emotional factor that can affect a boy's motivation is often referred to as pecking order. Pecking order refers to a boy's social standing among his peers. Boys who are high in the pecking order often fit common definitions of masculinity (physically mature, athletic, etc.), as well as possessing strong leadership and verbal skills. Boys who are low in the pecking order are more often the boys who enter puberty later and who are smaller and less athletic—not fitting the standard definitions of masculinity and more likely to be bullied (Gurian, 2010).

As teachers, this should concern us. Students who have lower social status among peers are under greater stress. Increased stress means a higher level of the stress hormone, cortisol, in the bloodstream. Elevated cortisol levels

> Boys are shame-phobic. Do not shame a boy in public. Shame reflects on who the boy is rather than what the boy has done. When you publicly shame a boy, you risk permanently losing his respect (Payne & Slocumb, 2011).

interfere with the brain's ability to learn new content and can contribute to behavioral problems, including making it more difficult for boys to sit still (Ruttle et al., 2011). Pecking order is also based on factors that a boy may be able to control, to some degree, such as mannerisms, values, style of dress, and so on—"the norm to conform" with peer group definitions of who and how one is supposed to be in the world.

A high school teacher told me a story that provides an excellent illustration of norming to peer culture. After math tests had been returned to students, one male student, who had scored very well on the test, came up to the teacher's desk and spoke in a hushed tone. "Please don't tell anyone what I got on this test." The teacher realized that this boy did not want his peers to know about his good test grade because it would hurt his social standing. He didn't want his peers to catch him "acting white." His teacher responded, "I'll make you a deal. You keep working hard, and I won't say a word!"

Doing well in school is often considered by boys as being incompatible with masculinity. School is something that girls do and, in their ongoing quest to reach alpha-male status, many boys don't want to draw attention to their academic efforts. In my own household (headed by two educator parents, nonetheless), I experienced this. While my son was supposedly doing his homework one evening, I saw that he kept stopping to text. Finally, I told him "Connor, tell them you are doing homework and have to go." It was both disappointing and informative when he replied: "Mom, you never say you're doing homework. You tell people you're blowing it off." Ah, how daunting the forces that conspire against us as parents and educators!

Another issue to be aware of is the practice of praising boys in front of their peers. Some boys, if praised in class, will intentionally misbehave in order to earn back the respect of their peers. But change environments and the opposite can be true. I observed boys in an all-boys high school English class responding eagerly to classroom instruction. When the teacher asked who wanted to read aloud, three-fourths of the hands in the room eagerly and urgently shot up in the air. For advocates of single-gender education, this is one of the examples cited for why all-boy classrooms work (Sax, 2009). Sensitivity to your students' peer culture is the key.

TRY THIS

As males, we don't want to look stupid, weak, or silly. We will keep quiet if any of those may be the outcome.

Jim Weber, vice principal, Mount Carmel High School

Those same boys who seem so tough are often the very ones who cry openly on the bench when they lose the championship game in overtime. Boys must feel safe as emotional beings in a setting where they do not pay the price for departing from the norm that they "man up."

Larry Hackett, teacher and educational consultant

Teaching an all-boys class is incredibly challenging, yet incredibly rewarding. Whenever the "light bulbs" go off in my boys' reading class, it is an amazing feeling. It happens for boys when they are willing to take risks and willing to reach out. It happens when boys feel comfortable with those around them and feel secure in their relationships within the class. Those special connections help boys grow with each other and within themselves.

Troy Rivera, reading instructor, University Middle School

Ability or Effort?

According to the National Association for Research in Science Teaching (Howe, 1996), boys and girls attribute different causes to their success. To a much greater extent, girls believe they succeed because they work hard. Boys are far more likely to believe they succeed because they are inherently bright. The implications of this research are very important, especially when students struggle and fail in school. A girl is more likely to tell herself, "You just need to study more next time," and this can serve to motivate her to work harder. Boys, however, are more likely to believe they aren't capable and say, "I am just dumb at reading" or "I can't write at all." Boys who attribute failure to a lack of ability are far less likely to believe that they can change the outcome by working harder. Given most boys' competitive nature, this rather deterministic view of themselves can make boys more prone to avoiding the tasks that they find difficult.

Sensitive Boys

Sensitive boys frequently do well in school, while not fitting the standard definition of maleness. They may prefer to spend their time reading and writing, or pursuing the arts. Or they may wear their emotions on their sleeve and have a heightened sense of justice and empathy. These can be wonderfully refreshing qualities in a boy or young man; however, he is far more likely to be the target of teasing and to be lower in the social pecking order.

Even though these boys may be doing well academically, don't let them fall off of your radar. They are struggling, just as much as the "tough guys," to figure out who they are and where they fit in. Opportunities for boys to see many definitions of being male—especially sensitive, empathic men through role models, mentors, literature, and film—help boys to find their purpose and be more confident in breaking the mold.

If you are looking for an excellent book on the topic of raising and educating sensitive boys, I recommend *The Strong,*

Sensitive Boy by Ted Zeff, PhD. It addresses a myriad of topics, including the sensitive boy's relationship with his mother and father, what to do if a dad can't connect with his sensitive son, supporting the sensitive boy at school and with making and keeping friends, playing sports, managing emotions, and the teen and young adult years. As you develop your professional and parent libraries, this is a good book to add to the collection.

Asking for Help

Just as many men don't stop to ask for directions, boys too often do not ask for academic help until it is too late. Sometimes boys aren't organized or forward-thinking enough to realize how their grade in a class is shaping up. Many boys don't check their grades online as often as they should. If their parents aren't checking either, they may really be out of the loop. They may not pay attention at the beginning of the term when you explain what percentage of their grade is based on homework and tests. A boy who is doing well on tests but not doing his homework (or vice-versa) may be totally blind-sided by his final grade. Others get behind and, instead of digging in and working harder, check out. Other boys feel that it is a sign of weakness to ask for help. Others aren't sure what to do, so they do nothing. Remember how boys are more likely to attribute failure to lack of ability? Society tells males that men are supposed to be strong and capable and to have all the answers. Admitting to a struggle—socially, emotionally, or academically—can be tough for a boy.

So What Can We Do?

These complex biological and societal dynamics mean that boys need to be supported socially and emotionally in some very thoughtful ways. Here are some strategies to consider:

- Challenge the myth of the tough guy. Reinforce with boys in your class that it's okay to show feelings (PBS Parents, n.d.a).

- Especially in the younger grades, help boys create a "feeling-word" dictionary/thesaurus that they can add to throughout the year. For older boys, this work is still important—and, in fact, it is absolutely critical for boys of poverty. Modify (for age-appropriateness) and implement the feeling-word thesaurus strategy for middle and high school boys (Payne & Slocumb, 2011).
- Invite male role models to class who are academically oriented.
- Don't scold boys publicly. It threatens their status in the pecking order and harms your relationship with them (Gurian, 2010).
- Be cautious of praising boys for academic achievements in front of the class if you believe that may cause embarrassment.
- Don't wait for boys to ask for help. Check in regularly with them and insist that they get help when needed (James, 2007). Insist on the use of planners and other academic and organization strategies provided in Chapter 6.
- It's not enough to tell boys that they can come in after school to get help and hope that they show up. Set a specific appointment time with boys.
- Consider creating single-gender advisory periods, which give adults time to address some of these boy-specific social-emotional issues. School counselors/psychologists should also consider creating single-gender student groups.

FORGING POSITIVE RELATIONSHIPS WITH BOYS

Teenagers look up to authority figures even if we say we do not.

Richard, age 16

Given that boys come to school generally being less affiliative, working harder to be tough and independent, talking less about feelings, and being driven by the opinions of their peers, it may seem like a real challenge to form quality relationships with boys. While we know it can be done and we are successful with a number of boys, too many are missing out on these human connections at school. We need to be prepared to go about relationship building in some different ways. Many relationship-building strategies are effective for both boys and girls, but some are particularly critical for boys. Consider how groups of girls interact and bond and then consider how groups of boys interact and bond. This can be a starting point for how we, as adults, may connect more meaningfully with boys.

Connecting With Any Boy . . . Even Hard-to-Reach Boys

One of my favorite experts in the area of effectively building relationships with youth from troubled backgrounds is Dr. Robert Brooks (2000; http://www.drrobertbrooks.com). He asks the very important question: "Why do some kids overcome their difficult, even abusive, circumstances and why do others not?"

Especially in high-poverty schools, we hear conversations in schools that go something like this, "Well, he just doesn't get the support he needs at home," "There are no good male role models in our community," or "These kids come from terrible homes. What difference can I make in six hours (or 48 minutes) a day?" Dr. Brooks's presentation of the research on high-risk youth is compelling. We *can* make a difference. Dr. Brooks presents research indicating that a young person's connection with a caring, trusted, and supportive adult is the key to resiliency and overcoming obstacles in life. A teacher is a commonly identified support system by young people, second only to a parent. And here we underestimate the power that we have to change lives at school!

Eric Jensen, in his book *Teaching With Poverty in Mind: What Being Poor Does to Kids' Brains and What Schools Can Do About It* (2009), states that "Poverty stunts the formation of healthy relationships" (p. 86). These children who are lacking in secure attachments often exhibit an "I don't need anyone's help" kind of attitude. These are the very children to whom we need to reach out and become that source of reliable support. Dropout rates decrease and achievement rises when positive bonds are formed between students and staff.

TRY THIS

- At a faculty meeting, introduce Dr. Robert Brooks's writings about "charismatic adults" (http://www.drrobertbrooks.com).
- Have teachers identify students who they think may not be able to identify an adult support person at school. Have teachers list student names.
- Have nonteaching staff consider this too.
- Take all student names, make note of duplicates, and create a list of identified students. If several adults identify the same student, this should increase the level of immediacy in the school's intervention.
- Discuss any concerns that exist for these students and why they may have been identified.
- Have faculty and staff members identify a student(s) on the list with whom they will connect and intervene.

The statistics make it clear—boys are more likely to be disengaged, unmotivated, and at risk of dropping out. They are less affiliative and, pressured by societal expectations regarding masculinity, are less likely to

> I love my history teacher because he relates to his students with stories of when he was our age.
>
> Adam, age 15

ask for help. Relationships with supportive adults are a critical factor in turning apathy and underachievement around. When students are identified as not having this point of connection at school, efforts must be redoubled to identify someone who will intentionally and supportively reach out and connect with the young person.

The key to connecting is simple. It is all about the small, caring gestures that take place on a daily basis. Here are some great examples:

- Greet students individually as they enter the classroom. Give high-fives and smiles. Don't be preoccupied with writing on the board or handing things out.
- Ask students about their outside activities and interests— "How was your game on Saturday, Jared?" When possible, attend student activities outside of school.
- Watch a football game over the weekend—or at least read up on it—so that you have something to talk to your students about on Monday (even if you can't stand football): "How 'bout them Redskins, Sam?"
- Learn about the students' pop culture interests so that you can discuss them with them. That means occasionally tuning into their music, TV shows, and films to educate yourself.
- Spend time walking around at break, recess, or passing periods to casually greet students and interact with them.
- Share stories from your own life (and as a child) so students can get to know you as a person.
- Have a sense of humor. Be willing to laugh at yourself and don't take yourself too seriously. Boys, in particular, don't respond well to teachers who are too "buttoned-up," overly serious, and/or strict to the point that they can't be responsive to a situation.
- As a principal, be out front of the school in the morning to individually welcome students into school for the day. Challenge yourself to learn student names— practice with old yearbooks and silently run through names whenever you are in a classroom. Wave off the school buses at the end of the day.
- Participate with students in PE classes once in a while, just for fun. This might include showing up for a little roller-skating, tennis, juggling, or even rock climbing. Drop in for the afternoon at the outdoor education camp or join staff and students on an occasional field trip.

- Mail a postcard to three students every week. Write a personal and positive note of kudos. Target students who you notice seem disconnected.
- For more ideas, check out this publication: *150 Ways to Show Kids You Care,* available from the Search Institute (n.d.; $11.95 for 20 copies).

Communicating With Boys

For many years, I described my son as monosyllabic. Answers to questions such as "How was your day?" and "Do you have any homework?" consisted of "fine," "no," and other one-syllable responses. So I laughed out loud when Michael Thompson, in *Raising Cain* said, "If you are willing to . . . not be disappointed by brief answers, you can communicate with boys." Knowing that this can be normal helps us relax—especially as parents! Don't give up on talking with boys even when the conversation seems mostly one-sided.

There are a few tricks to drawing boys out of their "monosyllabicism!"

- Ask boys their opinions and listen respectfully and openly to what they have to say.
- Allow them to feel that they are an authority on some issues. Talk about things on which he can be an "expert."
- Engage the boy in a friendly verbal challenge or debate on an issue—not from a position of authoritativeness but from a position of playfulness. He'll love the challenge.
- Learn about a boy's interests so that you can engage him in conversations. Is he into March Madness? Find out who's playing, who's picked to win the series, and use this as a launching point for getting a boy talking. Before you know it, the door is open for conversations about a wider variety of topics.

Another strategy, offered by Cathy O'Donnell of Black Rock Elementary School in Erie, Colorado, is to focus conversations more on "doing" and "thinking" rather than "feeling," in order to draw boys out. She shares, "I try to use the word 'think' more than 'feel' when processing with many of the boys. I listen for which verb they use and then incorporate it into my questions such as, 'What did the other boy think when you said that?' or 'How do you think your choice to do that helped or hurt the situation?'"

Get Moving

Whereas girls may gravitate to sitting together to talk, boys tend to open up when on the move. When you want to chat, go for a walk instead of sitting down. Pass a ball as you devise a plan. Build something or take it apart—and talk as you work with your hands. Even if no words are exchanged, spending time with a boy doing something physical, such as joining in a game of four-square at recess, can create an important inroad. Movement reduces stress, increases a sense of well-being, and increases blood flow and oxygen to the brain (E. Jensen, 2000a)—all wonderful conditions for forming connections, building trust, and opening lines of communication.

Use Humor

I had the privilege of working with a dynamic and energetic male teacher in the past year who teaches an all-boys eighth-grade class. Now if that job doesn't require a sense of humor, I don't know what does! He gave me a list of all the things that a teacher needs to be. Topping that list? Comedian. Some of the time, that means being able to find the humor in the situations and the topics that present themselves. In many other cases, it means being able to appreciate the boys' sometimes edgy or slapstick brand of humor. There is no better strategy for connecting with a boy than laughter, and boys have a way of presenting plenty of opportunities for a light moment—that is, if you can be relaxed enough to perceive it as that. With boys, in particular, humor plays an important role and is an essential vehicle for relationship building, communication, and learning itself.

Sandy Lubert, a middle school teacher and mother of three boys (as well as sister to three older brothers), has extensive firsthand personal and professional experience with males and the central role of humor in their lives. Sandy shares:

> As a mum and teacher, I have seen that many adolescent boys lack confidence, emotionally and socially. They often struggle to understand—let alone define and/or communicate—their needs and feelings. My own sons are 13, 15, and 17, and I can say honestly that if it weren't for humor, there would be very little interaction at all in our family! Frequently unsure of themselves with teenaged girls and serious conversation of any kind, these guys definitely know what they like, and are happy to share it, when it comes to funny!
>
> Boys don't just enjoy humor, they rely on it. They need it to shield them from the pain of angst and social awkwardness; they use it as an oar to navigate the sometimes choppy and uncertain waters of responsibility, relationship, and intimacy. At a loss for (appropriate) words, they can always resort to, "A funny thing happened . . ."
>
> In the classroom, humor offers boys a safety net so that they can take risks and step outside of their (often narrow) comfort zones. Saving face is crucial. If and when a boy stumbles—literally or metaphorically—he can fall back into humor and, like bowing after a pratfall, laugh at himself. As an educator, it is imperative that you open this door for your male students. Let them know you're comfortable with humor. Laugh with them. Whenever possible, incorporate comedy into your lessons, curriculum, and assignment options. The relief your male students feel will be visible and palpable. I have witnessed many of the most reluctant learners step through this open door into growth and learning.

Who Is This Teacher of Boys?

I have had the pleasure of conducting teacher workshops with Tim Coble, teacher and department head of World

> Show interest in the quirky humor, the original perspectives of boys.
>
> Ralph Fletcher, author of *Guy-Write: What Every Guy Writer Needs to Know* and *Boy Writers: Reclaiming Their Voices*

Languages at the K–12 American School of Doha in Qatar. Tim has dedicated extensive time to the study of gender-differentiated teaching techniques. He boils down relationship building with boys to some very important tenets for teachers. I can envision a wonderful faculty discussion about each of these bullet points, in terms of what each of Tim's points means and what each would look like if it were operationalized in a school or classroom. What else would your school add to this list?

- Be organized and competent.
- Be a man (or woman) of your word. Be demanding and fair.
- Offer consequences, never threats, and stick to them.
- Be ready to play—with boundaries.
- Cry when not crying would be inhuman.
- Be a model of behavior and self-understanding.

WHAT EDUCATORS HAVE TO SAY ABOUT BUILDING RELATIONSHIPS

I also make sure that I know the sports scores and all that is happening in their world . . . at least as much as I can. During their break time, I circulate and try to discuss intelligently the latest movies or the best prospects for winning the NBA, NHL, or MLB championships—it always pays off a hundredfold!

Elementary school principal

Our day always starts with Morning Meeting, where students can share news from their life. Boys often share about winning the big game, their dog that threw up in the house, or something silly that a younger sibling did. Being able to laugh about these stories at 8 o'clock each morning helps boys to see our classroom as a welcoming place for them.

Stephanie Van Horn, fifth-grade teacher, Douglass Elementary School

Use humor, be fair, and link the curriculum to their passions (video games, sports, music, etc.), and most important, show each boy that you believe in them.

Eighth-grade all-boys class teacher

Understand their current pop culture—what's popular with them and why. Find out who their role model is. You can relate anything they're interested in and weave it into the curriculum. It's not about being hip. It's about taking time to get to know them and what they like.

Denise Savidge, academic dean, Cherokee Creek Boys' School

Sometimes adding "boy" humor allows boys to view teachers as more human. Also, watching the boys in their extracurricular activities and commenting on them helps to bond the students to teachers.

Rob Kodama, director of admissions and teacher, Crespi Carmelite High School

Share things about yourself that boys want to know, like "Who is your favorite football team?" If your boys like karate and you don't know about karate, have one of them teach you about it.

Vermelle Greene, principal/founder (retired), SACRED Life Boys Academy

MALE MENTORING AND ROLE MODELS

It's important to help boys to understand that the standards of manhood are not defined by street culture. Manhood should be defined by a set of values—a man is a person who understands himself and others, who cares for his family emotionally and financially.

Geoffrey Canada, president of the Harlem Children's Zone

Mentoring and role-modeling for boys and young men can take place in many different ways. One way is for teachers to bring male volunteers and guest speakers into the classroom. Sometimes, these mentors can be students' fathers. Other mentoring relationships can be informal relationships formed from within the building, such as a staff member making a special effort to reach out to a struggling student—taking time to talk, having lunch together, or joining in on recess. Other mentoring relationships are more formal, such as community-based partnerships that are organized through outside organizations like Big Brothers, private businesses, or a local university.

Sometimes, a formal mentoring curriculum is offered at school. While a formal Rites-of-Passage program—such as one offered as a unit within a course, as part of an advisory program, or during a weekend wilderness experience—is more common in private schools, it deserves consideration in the public sector as well. This is a time when single-gender settings can be invaluable. In an all-boys setting, boys can experience greater freedom to explore their journey from boyhood to manhood.

One place where single-gender mentoring is happening is in the Oakland Unified School District. In collaboration with the African American Male Achievement (AAMA) organization, high schools have instituted manhood development classes. Entering ninth-graders form a class that meets daily and stays together for all four years of high school. Using the 180 Curriculum (http://180-degrees.com/) as a basis, the manhood development class teaches students about topics ranging from proper dress and filling out a job application to study skills and public speaking. One of these classes is taught by Tiago Robinson at Oakland High School. Mr. Robinson himself grew up on the inner-city streets of Oakland. By

> There are times when we are laughing, and there are times when we are shedding tears together. Knowing the streets and where they come from is the biggest thing in building a relationship with these boys. Sometimes you need to set down the lesson plan and understand what's going on in their lives.
>
> Tiago Robinson, teacher of a manhood development class, Oakland High School

ninth grade, he had dropped out of high school and was doing what he calls "a lot of bad stuff." Relationships, family, and high expectations helped him overcome a life of crime to earn a master's degree and become a teacher. Now, standing in front of the young men who are growing up on the same tough streets as he did, Mr. Robinson has powerful credibility. "You can rise above your circumstances," he says to them. "I had to stay out of trouble and, believe me, that was hard to do. Work hard, you're smart, keep your eye on the prize."

As a "boy" teacher, I've always believed that boys need more positive male role models in their lives. They have sports figures who excel at outcompeting others and tend to be excused for poor behavior more than they should. They have other models, including the military and business leaders, who also are considered to be successful if they outmuscle and outhustle others. As much as our society steers boys toward outcompeting and outdoing others, boys need nurturing, especially from adult males. They need to be encouraged and allowed to develop their emotional selves. Schools need to find ways to involve positive adult males in the lives of boys.

Kenneth Nova, fifth-grade teacher, Douglass Elementary School

A Mentoring Curriculum

There are many guideposts for mentoring programs, but I especially respect and recommend the work of Michael Gurian. During his teen years, Gurian's father worked on the Southern Ute reservation in Colorado, and Gurian spent a great deal of time on the reservations himself. These early learnings about Vision Quest and the sweat lodge profoundly impacted his philosophies. Gurian went on to study natural elements in youth development, holistic and spiritual quests, and adolescent rites of passage.

In *A Fine Young Man: What Parents, Mentors, and Educators Can Do to Shape Adolescent Boys Into Exceptional Men,* Michael

Gurian (1999) explores the coming-of-age mentoring process of adolescent boys from a historical perspective. A powerful model introduced in the book is called the Core of Manhood. It organizes mentoring into four key themes or values that mentors can use to structure and guide their relationship with the young person.

C . . . Compassion

O . . . Honor

R . . . Responsibility

E . . . Enterprise

Having a framework of common language and themes, such as the Core of Manhood model, gives mentors a foundation of values from which their relationship can grow. Gurian recommends conversation-starters that stimulate dialogue about character building and the characteristics of responsible manhood:

"How did you show compassion today?"

"What does it mean to have honor?"

"What have you been responsible for today?"

"What is something enterprising that you have you done?"

Another important component of mentoring is what the mentor and mentee do together. As movement-oriented as boys' bodies and minds are, the best way to mentor is to talk while "doing" rather than sitting. Michael Thompson, coauthor of *Raising Cain*, recommends that mentors "work alongside him doing something challenging, something meaningful where he can make a contribution and see it. In that shoulder-to-shoulder setting, close relationships grow quickly." Michael Thompson's recommendation is perfectly embodied by an elementary school principal's practice in Ontario, Canada:

I garden with them. I have found particularly over the past two years that establishing relationships while gardening on our school property has paid huge dividends. I sometimes give points for the longest weed pulled or the most weeds pulled or the hardest worker. I get to know the boys this way. Just like any other kid, they want you to know them by name and know something about them. While we are gardening I get a chance to do this.

Finding Role Models

Education needs a few good men. According to the U.S. Bureau of Labor Statistics' 2011 Current Population Survey, males comprise 2.3% of preschool and kindergarten teachers and 18.3% of elementary and middle school teachers—a dip from 2007 numbers. High school is better with, on average, 42% male teachers. We need boys to be exposed to more men who value education and can be role models in the areas of reading and writing—just as girls have been exposed to women in the science and math arenas. Here are some suggestions for getting more male role models into your school:

> A strong single-sex advisory program with male advisors can make such a difference for boys. When boys can sit together, play together, share information together, and have an adult male role model who takes them under his wing, great things happen.
>
> Peggy Daniels, principal, Carolina Day Middle School

- In the literacy/language arts classrooms, request that each father (or an older male family member) commit to coming into the classroom one time during the school year. This is only a 20- to 30-minute time commitment on the father's part. Have the fathers do a book talk, share a piece of their own writing for student critique, or discuss how they use reading or writing in their professional work.

- Invite a male staff member from your school to lead a book talk, read aloud, conduct writing conferences, or engage with students in other literacy-related activities. Identify other family members who don't live close by but are willing to help. Grandfathers, uncles, and other male family members can videoconference with your students to discuss a piece of student writing or do a read-aloud.

- Identify men at the central office or on the school's board who will agree to serve as a one-on-one male role model for one or more boys during the school year. This relationship can consist of notes, phone calls, and regularly scheduled visits. Don't overlook staff members like bus drivers and custodians in your school. All adults can be called upon to reach out to students.

- In the elementary grades, set up classroom buddies with another class. Pair boys with boys and girls with girls to provide opportunities for same-sex mentoring. Have boys read and write with and for one another. Have them develop recommended book lists to share with other boy pairs.

- Post students' writing on a wiki (an online platform that can be updated by any user). Request that parents read student writing and leave occasional comments. Be specific with the dads! Assign them a week during the school year in which they read and respond to one piece of student writing per day.

TRY THIS

While most people in the community recognize the importance of providing boys with male role models, many have not stopped to consider the urgency of doing so and what can be done. During a Back-to-School or other parent informational event, have parents view the *60 Minutes* segment called "The Delinquents" (2001), which is available for purchase (http://www.gurianinstitute.com). This powerful 15-minute video generates urgency to get men involved in young boys' lives. Additionally, the video stimulates discussion and problem solving about how the school and community can work together to accomplish this.

THE FINAL BUZZER

Quality learning can't begin if students' social and emotional needs are not addressed first. Both biological and sociological factors influence boys' attitudes, communication styles, emotional literacy skills, and motivation in school. Understanding the social-emotional and relational needs of boys can help us build those critical relationships.

> As educators we need to understand and be part of the journey from a boy to manhood.
>
> Edward Ybarra, principal, Central Catholic High School
>
> In my manhood development class, we create a culture of understanding. Getting the boys connecting is key. They ask me, "Do you trust us?" and I say "Yes—I trust you." With trust and relationships, anything is possible.
>
> Tiago Robinson, teacher, Oakland High School

- For boys more than girls, the quality of the teacher-student relationship affects their attitude and work ethic at school.
- Not all boys have that tough exterior. We have to support the sensitive boys too.
- When boys fail to ask for help, they need adults who are tuned in and ready to reach out.
- Mentoring programs and role models can help guide boys to responsible manhood, while debunking the myths about masculinity and "what makes a man."
- When it comes to finding male role models for boys, have an "all hands on deck" philosophy that includes parents, community members, and staff at the school site and district/board level.
- Boy-friendly communication strategies can get even the most "strong and silent" types to open up and start talking.
- Connecting with boys requires knowing what your boys like, enjoying their sense of humor, and being active.

Boys want and need structure, humor, and a relationship with someone who they trust to do what is right by them even if, at times, it's painful.

Eighth-grade all-boys class teacher

Additional materials and resources related to *Writing the Playbook: A Practitioner's Guide to Creating a Boy-Friendly School* can be found at www.boyfriendlyschools.com. Kelley King can be reached at kelleykingpd@hotmail.com.

The Ground Game

Setting Up Classrooms That Help Boys Succeed

Prohibited from the physical activity they need and criticized for the content of their minds, it is not surprising that some of these boys get off to a bad start, giving up before they have even begun.

Jane Katch, kindergarten teacher and author of *Under Deadman's Skin: Discovering the Meaning of Children's Violence Play*

L et's face it—teaching boys can be fun. The very things that are maddening about boys—their energy, their out-of-the-box thinking, their sense of humor—are the very things that crack us up and make us love them. No one makes me appreciate the joy of teaching boys more than one particular all-boys high school teacher in Texas. Laughter is commonplace in her classroom, and her energy matches the energy of the students. She's just as quick with a comeback as are the young men seated in front of her. Instead of trying to control her male students' behavior, she expertly rides the contours of it, while getting the work done.

Most of us who have spent any time in the field have a number of stories about our experiences working with boys and young men. Larry Hackett, a longtime Minnesota educator for students ranging from elementary age through college age, recalls the days of the open-concept classroom and what he learned about the most productive kind of environment for his male students:

> The boys in my class were in agony. In our third-grade open classrooms, the usual hubbub of learning was severely discouraged. Teachers were constantly "shushing," and time-outs were being handed out left and right. But three particular days in April proved to be liberating. We divided the class and moved the boys to a relatively soundproof gym storeroom. It was an experiment (perhaps out of desperation) that yielded some remarkable results. In our "cave," sitting and rolling and standing on our heads and reclining and resting on tumbling mats, we studied and shared and learned. There were no trips to the principal's office on those days. Time-outs were nonexistent. I couldn't believe the difference in our productivity. I realized right then how important it is for these boys to be able to "be in their bodies" and to make "joyful noises" if they are to rediscover the joys of learning.

So, with appreciation for all those boys in our lives who challenge us and warm our hearts—the following classroom characteristics and practices are particularly well suited to helping those fidgety, energetic, humorous, risk-taking, and spirited boys survive and thrive in our classrooms. And don't forget the girls! Just because they are more neurologically tolerant of a sit-n-git, lecture-oriented classroom doesn't mean that it is an effective way for them to learn. Changing your classroom and your instruction for the benefit of boys will do wonders for the girls.

Use this chapter to conduct a thorough inventory of current classroom practice. What is in place? What needs to be added or reworked? What should be required schoolwide, and what should be at individual teacher discretion? What professional development, materials, resources, or teacher characteristics/skills are needed?

At the beginning of the year, this chapter can serve as the basis for a combined day of professional learning time (for reading and discussion), followed by teacher work time (for classroom setup). Throughout the year, this chapter can be used to help teachers develop and monitor professional goals and as the discussion content for PLC meetings. Recommendations from this chapter can be incorporated into existing classroom walk-through checklists and "look fors." Finally, these lists can be an invaluable tool during Response to Intervention (student support) meetings to help interdisciplinary teams identify new ways to support struggling students (most of whom, let's not forget, are boys!).

TRY THIS

Have grade-level or departmental teams become "experts" on the implementation of one or more recommendations from this chapter by doing more research and trying it out in their own classrooms. Have them make a staff presentation that explains how the strategy has worked for their students, along with recommended variations or adaptations, and sources for any teacher-made or purchased materials.

PHYSICAL ARRANGEMENT OF THE CLASSROOM

Seating Arrangements

Creating a brain-based, boy-friendly (and girl-friendly!) classroom means decreasing the use of the "chairs-in-rows" setup. Make sure classrooms are conducive to student movement, collaboration, and projects.

- Boys tend to need a little more physical space in a classroom. A table setting that works well for four girls may be too crowded for four boys. Put two to three boys at the table, if space allows (Blundin, 2010).
- Space desks apart adequately, especially at the younger grades. Boys often have a hard time keeping their hands to themselves, so this can help reduce the problem (James, 2007).
- Boys, especially, benefit by exposure to natural outdoor light, as well as more brightly lit indoor conditions (Knez, 1995). To the extent possible, consider seating some of your higher-need boys closer to windows (assuming that things outside the windows don't pose an additional distraction) or where artificial lighting is the brightest in the room.
- Boys have more difficulty hearing the higher register and softer tone of the female voice (Sax, 2005). With a female teacher, especially, some boys may need to be seated closer to the front of the classroom.
- Boys are more alert when they are standing than sitting (Sax, 2011). Provide "standing stations" in the room where students can stand and work. A podium or a classroom surface of appropriate height can serve this purpose, or a specially built standing desk can be purchased. Often, a regular student desk can be modified with longer legs. During lectures, designate spots in the room where students have the option of standing while listening. During one-on-one assessments or conferences with students, allow the boy the option of standing up.
- Provide modifications to traditional chairs that allow boys to have some movement while sitting. The idea is to provide students with an outlet for movement, instead of trying to squelch it (Jacket, 2010; Schilling, 2006). Occupational therapists are experts in this area and can provide you with research-based strategies, activity ideas, and equipment. Examples include:

- Therapy bands (those colorful stretchy lengths of rubbery material used in physical therapy) can be tied between the front two legs of a chair. Students can push down or back on the therapy band with their heels to get some movement.
- Wedge or gel seats. These were frequently used in my school. They allow students to wiggle and shift more in their seats.
- Some newer chair models are constructed with a base that allows for some backward rocking motion without risk of tipping.
- One-legged stools, sometimes called "focus stools." These are similar to core fitness balls in that they allow some rocking. These can be purchased or handmade by a willing volunteer (see Figure. 6.1).

Figure 6.1

○ Acquire a class set of clipboards so that students can take a clipboard and move anywhere in the classroom to work (Bright, n.d.). This can include a carpeted area, a bean bag chair, or a few stadium seats placed on the floor.

> On average, girls can handle a sedentary school day, although it is not good for them. But boys need movement to survive.
>
> Dr. Kenneth Ginsburg, professor of pediatrics at the University of Pennsylvania's School of Medicine, excerpted from *The Trouble with Boys: A Surprising Report Card on Our Boys, Their Problems at School, and What Parents and Educators Must Do* (Tyre, 2006).

Classroom Decoration

Visual resources are helpful for boys in the classroom; however, it's not good to create an overly cluttered visual environment (James, 2007). Here are some recommendations:

- Relevant information that is displayed with clean lines and strong contrast is most helpful. A lot of extraneous information and decoration can be distracting.
- Primary colors work well for boys since they see those colors better. Subtle color variations, such as the variation between pastels, are more difficult for boys to discern.
- Make sure you designate a visible place in the room that lists homework. On this same wall, it can be helpful to have hanging folders or slots where handouts from lessons are kept. That way, if a student misses class, he is able to get the handouts easily (without asking for help. . . . remember the students who are less likely to ask for what they need? The boys!).

Lighting

Healthy brain development, school success, and mood are all enhanced through exposure to outdoor natural light (Edwards & Torcellini, 2002). Further, sunlight increases serotonin levels, which helps decrease many symptoms of attention deficit disorder (Kuo & Taylor, 2004).

- Get students outdoors for learning as much as possible. This is also a case for recess and outdoor breaks!
- There's a correlation between student achievement and the quality of the physical environment—including lighting. Mimicking real, natural light (such as full-spectrum lighting) is better than standard fluorescent lighting (National Institute of Building Sciences, 2012). Further, boys perform better (problem solving, long-term recall, and mood) under cooler 4000K lights, while girls perform better under warmer 3000K lighting (Knez, 1995).

> My university training did not prepare me for the different ways that boys and girls learn! Fortunately, I was able to follow my intuition about what the boys need. Our school was on a farm property, and there were lots of opportunities to be outside—we ran and walked fence rails every morning, in addition to an "obstacle course" of activities—balancing, rolling, jumping, and tossing activities. Even with so much movement before coming into the classroom, I still needed to create opportunities within the lessons and during the day for kids to be up and active.
>
> Janet Allison, founder of Boys Alive!, director of the Gurian Institute Parenting Division, and veteran Waldorf teacher

Classroom and School Libraries

If you are an elementary classroom teacher or a secondary language arts teacher, it is absolutely essential to have a classroom library that is appropriately balanced to suit the interests of boys and girls. Often,

> Kids are like plants: they need water and dirt and sun.
>
> Anonymous

classroom libraries are out of balance with more books that appeal to the girls (Moloney, 2002). Check out http://www.guysread.com and http://www.gettingboystoread.com for these and more recommendations:

- Take an inventory of your current selection of books to see where your classroom library stands.
- Be sure to include plenty of books that are nonfiction and action-oriented and that feature men as positive role models. Also, include books that are gross, edgy, and funny, as well as those that address your particular students' interests and passions.
- Classrooms should also offer nontraditional texts, such as graphic novels, game strategy manuals, and magazines (cars, snowboarding, videogaming, etc.)
- The next time you are placing a book order, have boys help select the books.
- Print off stickers and bookmarks from http://www.guysread.com so that boys can recommend their favorite books to other boys.
- Look for graphic novel adaptations of literary classics. Jonathan Wright, a middle school language arts teacher, offers students the graphic version first and then has students move to the traditional text with great success.
- Take advantage of boys' respect for older males. Invite older boys from your school or a neighboring school to do a book talk in your classroom (and make sure to order the book for your classroom library). Elementary schools often have "classroom buddies" set up between grade levels. Add a new twist by pairing kids with a same-gender classroom buddy and letting the students read and write together.

Fidgets

Offer busy boys and young men something to hold while they listen or otherwise need to be sedentary. The squeezing/fiddling action provides an outlet for fidgety energy and can help boys stay more alert (Rappaport, Bolden, Sarver, & Alderson, 2009; Schilling, 2006).

> In order to be successful, boys seem to thrive in an active, dynamic, and even somewhat seemingly chaotic classroom. The stereotypical quiet classroom with everyone seated at desks busily working away doesn't tend to keep boys motivated, engaged, or achieving at high levels. The key with boys is to make sure that they are "doing" as often as possible.
>
> Jonathan Wright, language arts teacher, Manhattan Middle School

- For younger children, it may be a squeezy toy with a wrist strap (so they don't drop it). For older boys, it can be a hacky-sack. I've seen teachers use a variety of appealing manipulatives, including "tangles," (balls of tangled plastic), a nut and bolt that boys can screw on and off, pipe cleaners to twist, and yarn for finger-knitting. Many options for kinesthetically appealing manipulatives can be found online, including this helpful website: http://www.trainerswarehouse.com/.

- Good teachers anticipate classroom management issues before they occur. Explain to boys how the "fidget tool" helps their brain stay focused (increased blood flow and oxygen). Then explain parameters for the fidget tool's use, such as "It can't leave your hands" and "Squeeze it in your lap or below the level of the table so that you don't distract others."

- Explain to boys that the fidget item is a "tool," not a "toy." That means it should be used to help learning, not distract from it. As with anything in the classroom, if it becomes a distraction, it goes away (until they're ready to try it again).

- Only the teacher can best determine where and when boys are able to use their fidgets. Some teachers allow it in circle time and reading groups. Other teachers confine the use of fidgets to independent seat work time.

- Some teachers provide individual fidgets to be kept in backpacks or desks. Other teachers provide a bucket of fidgets and allow students to get up and get one as students feel it is needed.
- At first, everyone wants to try something "new." The novelty will wear off and so will student use. At that time, you can encourage the students who need the fidget the most to continue using it.

Water Station

Water helps the brain learn and grow while improving mood and working memory (Ganio et al., 2011). Most people are chronically dehydrated. Don't let this happen to your learners.

- Provide students with regular access to drinking water throughout the day. A middle school teacher I know refills a large water jug and has students put their names on plastic cups with permanent markers for reuse. This eliminates the issue of students bringing in their own "clear liquids." Elementary schools often allow students to bring their own water bottles.
- During more stressful situations, such as during testing or during a behavioral incident, water is especially critical to improving student performance.

Technology

Technology can increase student interest and motivation, as well as expanding opportunities for students to collaborate with others and share their work with a larger audience (Mouza, 2008).

- Equip computers in your classroom with Skype, FaceTime, or other videoconferencing software. Allow students to work with remote peers or experts on their work. Additionally, videoconferencing can provide students with a larger audience for sharing their work—especially critical for boys for whom motivation is a challenge.

- Create a few PowerPoint slide shows that contain pictures depicting students' interests. When students can't think of anything to write about, they can open the slide show for some ideas, or it can be projected and put in slide show mode during writing time. Pictures—especially action-filled ones—can stimulate the thinking of highly visual-spatial learners.
- Set up a Listening Center with MP3 players and headphones:
  o Create playlists of background music suitable for listening during different types of activities. Students can choose to listen during independent seat work. See Chapter 7 for music resources.
  o Load MP3 players with teacher- or student-created podcasts. These podcasts can be a review of prior lessons, or they can be a student's report on a topic or a book report. These can be used to help students review old information, learn new information, or catch up on content if they missed school. Excellent high school podcast examples can be found on teacher Ben Boyer's biology website: http://schools.bvsd.org/p12/boulder/faculty/boyer/default.aspx.
  o Create a wiki or use GoogleDocs so that students can post their writing and other students can read and respond to it. This is simply a more tech-savvy and engaging way of having students do peer-editing, and it can be done anytime, anywhere, as long as students have the ability to log on. I see this kind of "editing in the Cloud" being used in more and more classrooms all the time.
  o Create a folder on your Promethean Board (if you are fortunate enough to have one) that contains a variety of multimedia files for "brain boosters" (read more about brain boosters in Chapter 7). These brain

booster files might contain a picture to cue a quick movement activity, or they could contain a video or music file.

Learning Centers

Learning Centers are *not* just for primary classrooms. Learning Centers offer students the opportunity to move around the classroom, collaborate with others, and review/reinforce the concepts in many different formats, as well as breaking up the longer class periods (in, for example, a block schedule).

- Learning Centers provide a break from lecture and can serve as a formative assessment tool.
- Some teachers create Learning Centers based on Gardner's Multiple Intelligences. This is a nice way to ensure that you include the cognitive learning preferences of both genders.
- Create some Learning Centers that use a game format and are competitive.
- It is possible to find some teacher blogs with helpful resources regarding Learning Centers in the middle and high schools, such as this one: http://forcur iousteachers.blogspot.com/2010/05/using-learning -centers-in-high-school.html.
- For Learning Centers at the primary level, be sure to include centers that offer fine-motor strengthening and dexterity activities, such as threading small items, fin-ger-knitting, playing jacks, picking up items with twee-zers or chopsticks, pushing coins through a slot, and so on. The goal is to enhance fine-motor and eye-hand coordination. Your school's occupational therapist can offer more suggestions. A quick online search for "fine motor strength activities" will provide you with many resources. Share these fun activities with parents via class newsletters or your class website so that they can work (and play!) with their sons at home.

- Offer "limited choice" so that boys can't spend all their time in one center or only the few centers that they choose.

CLASSROOM PROCEDURES

Schedule Considerations (elementary)

Structuring the school day in a brain-friendly way goes a long way toward accomplishing your goals.

> If you happen to be involved in new building construction or capital improvements in an existing building, be sure to check out the resources and recommendations at National Clearinghouse for Educational Facilities (http://www.ncef.org)

- Conduct morning meetings. These provide an opportunity for relationship building through personal stories and "check-ins" (Bechtel, 2004). Play music during morning meetings because it wakes up both hemispheres of the brain.
- Literacy blocks should be structured so that students have the opportunity for variety and movement. Long periods of sitting are deadly, especially for boys.
- Many teachers report that the popular elementary school "Daily Five" (http://www.dailyfive.com) routine for literacy/language arts time works wonderfully to meet the needs of boys for variety and movement during an extended instructional block.
- Don't forget recess. The exposure to fresh air, sunlight, and physical activity helps students process and retain what they have just learned. They will have greater readiness for learning once they return to the classroom.

Schedule Considerations (secondary)

A few brain-friendly scheduling considerations can help keep boys alert and engaged throughout the day.

- Block scheduling has become more common; however, teaching practices must change if block scheduling is to work. Teachers must incorporate more social interaction, more project-based learning, and more kinesthetic learning experiences. Lecturing for 90 minutes will ensure that block scheduling is disastrous to boys' engagement and learning.
- Block scheduling reduces the number of transitions in a boy's day, which is helpful for the male neurological system (Gurian & Stevens, 2005).
- Weekly advisory periods help keep students on track and keep them connected with a caring adult outside of the academic settings. Single-gender advisory periods allow for some wonderful mentoring and coming-of-age conversations (Gurian, Stevens, & Daniels, 2009).
- Build a 15-minute break into the morning, if possible. Having a little mental downtime helps students store what they have just learned and be more alert for the next class.

Goal Setting

Part of being competitive (as many boys are) is being focused on achieving a goal. Use that to your benefit by collaboratively setting short- and long-term goals for your boys (Center on Education Policy, 2012).

> Boys also need clear goals set for them so that they know how to achieve at high levels and what high achievement looks like. Making rubrics as a class, developing goals together with students, and showing the big picture before teaching the smaller parts can help boys feel successful and responsible for their learning.
>
> Stephanie Van Horn, fifth-grade teacher, Douglass Elementary School

- Goals can be organizational, behavioral, or academic in nature.
- Have boys chart their goals visually, as well as their progress toward their goals.

- Incorporate individual goals into team goals for the purpose of creating some friendly competition in class.
- Provide regular feedback to students to reinforce their efforts and create excitement around achieving their goals.

Creating and Enforcing Rules

Collaborate with students on the development of a few basic rules. Boys, especially, need to feel buy-in (Wanless, Patton, Rimm-Kaufman, & Deutsch, 2012).

- If a rule needs to be revisited, be open to that. Boys do not respond well to teachers who they perceive as "up-tight," unresponsive, or inflexible.
- Anticipate trouble spots for boys and spend sufficient time practicing/reviewing the procedures, especially as related to transitions and movement.
- Redirect disruptions with a little humor. A laugh can often defuse a student. Don't confuse humor with sarcasm, though.
- Boys need to know who is the "alpha." On the other hand, statements such as "I don't want to hear your excuse" can lead to resentment. Be flexible, but firm.
- Avoid confrontations with boys in front of other students.

> Helpful Classroom Management Web Resources
> http://www.theteachersguide.com/ClassManagement.htm
> http://www.educationworld.com/a_curr/archives/classroom_management.shtml
> http://www.teachervision.fen.com/classroom-management/resource/5776.html
> http://www.nea.org/tools/ClassroomManagement.html
> http://www.loveandlogic.com/
> http://www.responsiveclassroom.org

> You must be direct with the boys. Hints and references do not work.
>
> ROTC Instructor

- No matter how well you plan for a movement or other fun activity, there will be a few boys/young men who can't manage themselves. Follow through with consequences then invite them to join in next time.
- Set aside team or department time to discuss classroom management challenges and strategies.

Routines vs. Novelty

Predictability and routine help the brain know what to expect and reduce stress. On the other hand, too much predictability decreases alertness, so it is important to find the right balance between predictability and unpredictability. Take into consideration the age of your students: Younger children require more predictability to feel safe, while teenagers crave the novelty that unpredictability offers (E. Jensen, 1998).

- Novelty, especially for the adolescent, wakes up the brain. Novelty is something new, unique, or unexpected that presents itself as being fun and interesting to students, not threatening.
- Some classrooms offer a variety of familiar learning activities (project-based activities, labs, lectures, centers, games, etc.), but not always in the same order or on any given day. Students benefit from the variety but enjoy the familiarity of the activities they know.
- Some classes have the routine of a weekly quiz on Fridays and standardized study packets to help them prepare. Knowing what to study and how to study for a test is an example of something that should be very predictable and routine. This is especially critical for boys, who frequently don't know *how* to study. Make test content and format as predictable as possible—no surprises in this area.
- Changing the arrangement of desks is a way to create novelty that one middle school teacher shared with me. He wanted to keep his students on their toes by occasionally surprising them with a change of scenery, so to speak.

- Take students outside for learning. The change of surroundings will shake the doldrums.

Time, Place, and Manner

Many of the things that boys do, while challenging at times, are not inherently bad. Nor is the boy bad. Often, the boy's behavior is simply executed at the wrong time or place or in the wrong manner. Sometimes a behavior that a boy gets in trouble for at school is perfectly acceptable in another setting.

> Humor is an essential element—they need to have fun. Structure is also essential. For that fun to be meaningful, it has to be in the context and the structure of a learning environment. That means a clear line is drawn that applies to every boy. Once they understand how far they can go, they relax and enjoy.
>
> Eighth-grade teacher of an all-boys class

- Teach boys to understand how time, place, and manner works. For example, relieving oneself outside is okay on a camping trip but not on a playground. Roughhousing is okay in the backyard with a willing playmate, but not in the lunch line. Can the boy think of other examples?
- Time, place, and manner applies to high school boys as well. For example, older boys can be prone to horseplay. The difference? The 15-year-old is more likely to be suspended than the 5-year-old. Talk to adolescent males about how time, place, and manner apply to their decisions as well—both in and out of school.
- Post the words "Time, Place, Manner" in the classroom. When boys run afoul of a school rule, ask them, "Is there a better time, place, or manner for this activity?"
- Help boys apply time, place, and manner to writing topics as well, by considering their audience. Some types of writing are appropriate in one setting and with one audience, but not in another setting with another audience.
- For more information on this topic, see Chapter 4.

Managing Transitions

It can be more difficult—neurologically speaking—for boys to change gears and make transitions (Gurian & Stevens, 2005). Accommodating this helps things go more smoothly.

- Boys tend to have greater single-task focus due to the compartmentalization and lateralization of mental processing. Therefore, they can become more absorbed in a task and have a harder time breaking away when it is time to stop.
- Give boys advance notice of a change in routine. Give both an auditory and verbal cue (e.g., flick lights). Sometimes it helps to touch a boy on the shoulder as you speak. Speaking into a boy's right hear helps his left brain process the factual information that you are giving him.
- Block scheduling allows for fewer transitions in a boy's day, and thus a greater ability to focus more deeply and with extended time on one task.

Giving Instructions

Female teachers, in particular, need to understand the implications for vocal quality and oral instructions in the classroom (Sax, 2006, 2011).

- Boys hear better when the speaker's voice is lower and louder.
- Avoid sing-songy vocal patterns with sentences that end on an up note or higher pitch.
- Be more to the point. The male brain appreciates brevity.
- It's okay to speak louder, but use a dynamic range in your voice to provide the listener with "ear candy" for the brain.
- Write instructions on the board and explain the first one or two steps. Keep the auditory information brief and then let the boys get busy with the task. Move around the room to check for understanding and to provide information about the next steps.

Activity and Noise Levels

Brain-friendly boys' classrooms are generally busier and noisier, due to more hands-on, collaborative, and movement-oriented activities. If you are a teacher who prefers a quiet environment, this can take some getting used to.

> Directions should be available as a resource but should not be gone through in detail. In general, men don't like to stop for or read directions, and boys are pretty much the same. The key is to monitor progress and offer suggestions if missteps are made.
>
> Jonathan Wright, language arts teacher, Manhattan Middle School

- Busy, active classrooms aren't necessarily poorly managed classrooms. The key to a well-managed classroom is how engaged students are in their learning—not whether or not they are sitting quietly in rows.
- It is important that parents and classroom supervisors understand the components of a brain-friendly, boy-friendly classroom. Communicate early and often about how learning takes place in your classroom and provide the research to substantiate it.
- As a teacher of boys, you will want to be more dynamic (active and louder) in your presentation style. Move around, be expressive with your body, vary your tempo and inflection, be dramatic and animated.
- At times, some students will need a quieter work environment. Provide a quieter work area and a bucket of headphones that students can access when needed.

Handling Learning Materials

Often, teachers create procedures to reduce student movement—when, in fact, we should be doing the opposite. Boys are better served by getting up to get

> Boys like loud, dramatic readings from literature.
>
> High school English teacher

their own supplies instead of staying seated during these transitions.

- Regularly, or as often as you can, ask students to get up and collect their own supplies instead of utilizing "Paper Passers." Have students turn in their own work instead of having a group member collect it. Just walking across the classroom helps wake up a sleepy brain.
- In an art classroom or other similar setting, set up the materials in one area instead of at the student workstations. Have students get up to get what they need as they need it. Some students will collect what they need in one trip. Others will take the opportunity to make multiple trips for supplies. This is a great way for students to differentiate the amount of movement they get in class. This is also a way to reduce unnecessary trips to the bathroom for kids who simply need a reason to get up and walk.

Organizational Strategies

Don't make this an afterthought. Plan on systematically and sequentially teaching organization, just as you do the curriculum (James, 2007).

- Boys must use a planner. Period. Provide them. Insist on them. Don't let boys slack off on the use of them. This habit starts early. Provide time in class for students to update their planners. The biggest mistake I see made in classrooms is giving the assignment as the bell rings. By that time, you've lost most of your boys.
- Paper day planners are going the way of the dinosaur. Be open to how technology can help in this area. If you have the discretion to allow cell phones in class for specific learning activities, consider allowing students to take a picture of the assignment board. Allow them to type notes in the notepad or calendar application on their phone. Tweet assignments. Update your class

website weekly or nightly with homework assignments, as well as the downloadable worksheets or slide show presentation that goes with the lesson.

- Consider recording class lectures on an MP3 player. These audio files can easily be uploaded to a website for students who were absent or those who wish to hear the lesson again. It is also helpful for support teachers and tutors to be able to hear the lesson.
- Be specific about how a boy is to organize his class binder. Tabs? Pocket folders? Sections? Don't leave this to chance.
- Make it a homework assignment one night per week that boys organize their binders or folders. Provide students with a laminated "rubric" for what constitutes an organized binder. Have peers check assignment notebooks and binders the next day in class. Stick to this routine. Routines are a part of being an organized person, so you are both modeling and teaching helpful practices for academic success.
- A boy's organizational ability is directly correlated to his grades. Time spent on teaching boys how to effectively use a planner, organize a binder, organize a backpack, and maintain a clean desk or locker is time well spent on his academic well-being.

Competition

Boys' natural desire to compete can be a great motivator. Use it. Healthy competition helps keep boys engaged, while helping girls to build confidence (Gurian, 2005).

- Incorporate game formats regularly. I observed a class of high school boys that was divided into two "football teams." They moved the ball up and down the field (it was drawn on the whiteboard) by answering the teacher's questions. I've seen other teachers play the "Jeopardy" game with students, complete with music and a downloadable, interactive "Jeopardy" game template. Simple or complex, games work.

- Similar to a game, but with a more extended format, are simulations. I am always amazed at the incredible simulations that are available for purchase at http://www.teachinteract.com. Simulations can be found in every content area and at every grade level. They bring together all of the positive elements of competition, relevancy, collaboration, and project-based learning.

> Competition itself lends purpose to an activity. When we think about it, nearly all sports are pretty pointless in terms of what's actually being accomplished; it's the thrill of the competition that makes the activity meaningful.
>
> Jonathan Wright, language arts teacher, Manhattan Middle School

> Competition is a good motivator. If the guys are in teams, they will strive to do their best to be victorious, no matter what they are learning about.
>
> Eighth-grade teacher of an all-boys class

- If your students struggle with being good sports, then this is all the more reason to create opportunities for competition in your classroom. It's a skill that needs to be taught and reinforced.
- Don't offer anything of value for winning (such as extra credit points). A team cheer or high-fives all around can suffice. The real prize is simply the fun of playing the game—and that can be enjoyed by everyone.

Student Collaboration

"Pro-social" environments literally enhance neurogenesis (brain cell production). These new cells support learning, memory, and mood regulation (E. Jensen, 2008).

- A desire for social interaction is natural. Don't suppress it. Incorporate it into the classroom activities.
- Don't allow random social grouping more than 10–20% of the time. Instead, use more intentional partnering and grouping of students.

- Students should spend about 50% of every school day interacting with one another.
- Simple ways of increasing social interaction include explaining what you heard to a partner, a walk-and-talk review, or playing a partner review game.
- Setting up a buddy system with another class is commonly done at the elementary level. These vertical mentors (older students paired with younger students) are a great way to foster collaboration, build relationships, and capitalize on the power of "pecking order" (see Chapter 5).

Get Male Role Models Into Classrooms

For both biological and sociological reasons, boys respond well to respected, older males. Find ways to increase your boys' access to them (check out Chapter 5 for an expanded discussion of this topic).

> Something that I like about school is how you are there with your friends. It makes it much more enjoyable and not as stressful when you study with a friend or can get help from a friend.
>
> Sam, age 15

- Extend invitations to students' fathers to visit the classroom to read aloud a favorite picture book, to share a piece of their own writing, or to talk about how they use literacy in their line of work.
- Invite older males (former students, members of a service club, college athletes, etc.) to your classroom to do book talks on their favorite books.
- Encourage respected males at your school, such as coaches, to find opportunities to talk with the boys they come in contact with about books they like.
- Pair up with another classroom so that students can have a class buddy (e.g., first graders buddy with fifth graders).

The Final Buzzer

A productive school year starts before students even enter the classroom. As principals, instructional coaches, and teachers, invest time and resources to create the optimal brain-friendly classroom right from the start for boys—and girls! Here are a few things that you might consider doing in the spring or fall to operationalize the best practices we've discussed here:

- If you are in a coed setting, help stakeholders understand that reworking classrooms to become more brain based and boy friendly benefits the girls as well as the boys. It's simple: Teach to a wider range of cognitive styles, and more children, regardless of gender, will benefit.
- Revisit school policies that may interfere with desired classroom practices. For example, school policy may prohibit taking students outside during class time (I've heard of this!), student use of cell phones for educational purposes during the school day, or overly restrictive web filtering that interferes with technology use. How can you better align school policies with classroom best practices?
- Provide grade-level or departmental teams time to evaluate what teachers are already doing and not doing from this chapter. Have teams report at least three changes they can make that they believe will have the most impact on student engagement and achievement. Follow up to ensure implementation.
- Have teachers take the staff on a classroom walkthrough to show something that they have done to create a more boy-friendly learning environment.
- Have teachers share their best ideas for classroom practice at faculty meetings. I always call this part of the meeting "GIFTS"—Great Ideas From Teachers. Make it a regular part of every meeting.

- Set professional goals with individual teachers that identify strategies from this chapter.
- Prioritize a small amount of funding per classroom, or identify grant sources, to acquire the needed classroom resources, such as fidgets, alternative seating, high-interest books, and so on.
- Stock the professional library with recommended books for staff.
- In staff newsletters/communiques, include ideas and "tips" from this chapter.

An excellent teacher is interesting when they talk. They make you laugh, and they make you think hard.

Gary, age 14

 Additional materials and resources related to *Writing the Playbook: A Practitioner's Guide to Creating a Boy-Friendly School* can be found at www.boyfriendlyschools.com. Kelley King can be reached at kelleykingpd@hotmail.com.

7

Hitting It Out of the Park

Game-Winning Instructional Strategies for Boys (and Girls!)

When my son Joseph was in high school, he spent 8 or 10 hours one weekend using a flip camera to film a ping-pong ball bouncing into a paper cup that was perched on a skateboard rolling by. He and his friend clipped together the very few times they actually filmed this happening and made a short film. I asked: "Joseph, are you guys doing this for homework or a class project?" Joseph looked at me dourly. "Dad, since when have I ever done anything this interesting in school?"

Ralph Fletcher, author of *Guy-Write: What Every Guy Writer Needs to Know* and *Boy Writers: Reclaiming Their Voices*

Why can't school be about cool stuff like skateboards and ping-pong balls? Imagine a math classroom using skateboards and ping-pong balls for teaching a constructivist lesson in time, rate, and distance. Physics students calculate acceleration, momentum, and energy. In a technical writing lesson, students write out the steps for making their contraption work. In digital media class, they record, edit, and create an instructional video set to music that is posted on the school or class website or that is shared with a sister school in another country. The possibilities are endless!

Most teachers are excited to embrace strategies that they know (both intuitively and experientially) will reignite and reenergize student learning. Everyone, however, harbors a few nagging concerns that can block or slow their implementation of best practice. There may be a few of you who are already thinking, "Sorry, but bouncing ping-pong balls around the room is taking it too far!" I implore you: Let's not shut doors before we've even got them open. In education, that happens far too often and freezes many schools in a state of inaction. It's important that school leaders help teachers keep their minds open by anticipating the objections and concerns right off the bat. It's also important for teachers to know that they have your support and encouragement to take risks and to try new things. Here are a few issues that I have heard voiced by teachers, along with my response:

Concern #1: "I don't need one more thing on my plate."

Boy-friendly strategies are not "one more thing." To stick with the dinner plate analogy, this work is about rearranging the plate and changing the portion sizes. It is about getting back to what many teachers used to do and gave up before high-stakes testing arrived. This work is also about looking at teaching and learning from a boy's or young man's perspective—which ultimately helps us reach more kids, including second-language students, special needs students, and girls with a male-brain learning style. Ultimately, it will make many aspects of a teacher's work easier and more enjoyable rather than harder: Discipline problems will go down, and motivation will go up.

Concern #2: "I barely have time to cover the curriculum as it is."

Many of these strategies do not require any additional instructional time (such as standing up during lectures or walking during a partner review). These are "substitution" strategies that are quick and easy to implement—you substitute standing for sitting, for example. Some of the strategies do require 2–3 minutes of class time, but they yield a tremendous bang for the buck in terms of engagement and retention—far more than what would be attained by lecture alone.

Concern #3: "The curriculum is restrictive and must be implemented with fidelity."

The curriculum, including the Common Core, dictates the essential skills for students to acquire. It does not dictate *how* it must be taught. With the shift to the higher-order thinking emphasis of the Common Core, activities that increase collaboration and problem solving around real-world issues are getting a fresh new look. And this is boy friendly! The instructional strategies that follow will enrich your work, not detract from it. Even the most prescriptive kinds of instructional programs (such as the scripted reading programs that have made their way into a number of elementary schools) can be made more brain and boy friendly. I challenge you to take a highlighter and mark all the things in this chapter that can be used during your most tightly scripted lessons—there is actually a lot!

Concern #4: "I have a very small classroom budget."

The vast majority of these strategies require no new materials. Many require none at all. Some things can be brought back to life or repurposed—an old CD collection and boom box, for example. I have gone to great effort to provide you with a number of free online resources. For those things you do need, some teachers ask for classroom donations in lieu of personal gifts at the holidays. Also, check out the website http://www .donorschoose.org as a means of getting connected with folks willing to help teachers with materials and supplies. Remember: The most important ingredient for successful implementation is teacher receptiveness and creativity—and those things require an open mind, not more money.

Concern #5: "I worry about losing control of my class."

In reality, behavior problems go down when teachers teach to both the body and brain, instead of to the "shoulders up." Make a deal with students—you can offer more fun, interactive classroom activities if they can follow directions and return to their seats quickly, for example. Use a stopwatch to challenge students to beat the clock and transition quickly between activities. Practicing proactive classroom management, teaching students about how the classroom activities help their brains, and providing students with choices will help students know where the boundaries are (boys need that!) and will help them develop a sense of ownership.

Concern #6: "I don't want to focus on boys to the detriment of girls."

So-called boy-friendly strategies enhance the achievement and motivation of *all* students—and that means the girls too! The bottom line is that boys push the envelope more and challenge us to think beyond the traditional delivery model. There are a number of boys who can't reach their potential or will outright fail without access to boy-friendly supports in the classroom— it's literally a "make it or break it" situation for them. For other boys and many of the girls, access to these strategies takes their achievement gains to the next level. Thank goodness for the boys who make us stretch—they are the ones who push us to improve and, in the process, to help all kids.

Perhaps you encounter other concerns expressed by teachers. Be patient, allow opportunities for teachers to explore any attitudes or beliefs that are blocking their progress, and continually bring faculty back to the data (including your own school's data) to keep that sense of urgency high.

The classroom is where the rubber hits the road. If your school is to become a boy-friendly school, the changes must happen in the classroom where the boys are. Boys' perceptions of school—and their level of engagement—are ultimately crafted through the quality of their interactions with the teacher and the content. The classroom is where it's at. We cannot miss this critical opportunity to reshape the educational outcomes for boys in even a single classroom.

Let's now proceed to explore strategies for more effective instructional delivery. There is no expectation that every teacher implement every strategy; rather, this chapter provides a wide menu of options from which teachers can choose to enhance the repertoire of strategies that they are already implementing. Help teachers celebrate the many things that they are already doing well from this chapter, and then help them prioritize the most important strategies that need to be implemented immediately and at future dates.

TRY THIS

1. Have teachers highlight instructional strategies in this chapter that they are already using regularly. Have them put an asterisk beside the three instructional strategies that they believe they highly implement.

2. Using a different color highlighter, have teachers highlight six to eight strategies that they believe would be particularly beneficial for their students but that they are not currently using (or using very minimally). Have teachers put a checkmark beside two to three of those strategies that they want to prioritize for implementation within the next month.

3. Make a poster for each type of strategy (e.g., "Movement," "Visual-Spatial," "Music," etc.) and hang these posters around the room. Have teachers gather at a station that corresponds with a strategy that they would like to start implementing. Discuss their questions and ideas for implementation with fellow teachers.

4. Additionally, create mixed groups of teachers. Have the teachers who are high implementers of a particular strategy meet with teachers who would like to start or expand implementation of the same strategy. Share tips and ask questions.

Lecture Strategies

The problem with lecturing is that it is not brain friendly and it is used to the exclusion of other, more effective teaching techniques. For boys, many of whom are visual and kinesthetic creatures, the "sit-still-and-listen" lecture can kill attentiveness, motivation, and, ultimately, learning. Consider also what research says about the impact of media on the brain: Extensive exposure to video games and television, "may promote development of brain systems that scan and shift attention at the expense of those that focus attention" (Jensen et al., 1997). Children's brains are becoming increasingly wired for new kinds of attention—and inattention—in this changing world.

We don't have to entirely eliminate lectures, but we do need to do them in a brain-friendly way. This is critical for boys, while being helpful for girls too. Studies show that lecturing brings on frequent lapses in attention, starting at just 4 minutes into a lecture and with subsequent attention lapses occurring every 7–9 minutes. By the end of the lecture, attention lapses are occurring every 2 minutes (Bunce, Flenx, & Neiles, 2010).

- Keep lectures short. At the high school level, lecture should be broken up with active and interactive activities every 10–20 minutes. Have students walk across the room and share what they've learned with a partner or draw a picture of the main points. At the upper elementary level, lecture only 10–15 minutes before giving students an active processing break. These times represent the outer limits for the brain's ability to attend without significant wandering of the mind.
- Allow students to hold an object while listening. Squeezing a foam ball or a stress ball has been shown to improve attitude, attention, and writing abilities (Stalvey & Brasell, 2006). For additional information about the use of stress balls, check out http://www.livestrong .com/article/232320-about-foam-stress-balls/.

- Chewing gum during a lecture (or during test taking) also helps keep the brain alert due to the rhythmic movement of the jaw (Onyper, 2011).
- Doodling while listening increases auditory retention by 29% (Andrade, 2010). It is an activity that keeps the brain active, while not requiring a lot of thought. One teacher shared with me that doing origami while listening helps him tremendously, and he has taught origami to his fourth-grade students!
- Allow students to stand in the back of the room during lecture. Some teachers even create "standing stations" where students can stand and take notes in the back of the room. Remember, the male neurological system is more alert when it is standing than when it is sitting. Some especially active boys may need to walk back and forth in the back of the room (Sax, 2005).
- Use a dynamic and animated voice to engage boys. Move around and gesture with your hands—your movements will attract and hold boys' attention. If you are recounting an event, such as in a history class, play up the action in the event. Boys' attention is captured by dramatic action sequences (James, 2007). Include personal stories in your lectures as well! It's important for you to be relatable.
- Find humor in your lessons and appreciate humor when it occurs spontaneously. Your ability to laugh and "roll with it" will endear you to your male students. Boys value a sense of humor—both their own and yours! For some amazingly fun "brain-friendly humor tips," go to: http://www.readingprof.com/papers/Brain-Friendly%20Strategies/7_Brain-Friendly%20Humor%20in%20the%20Classroom%20(map).pdf.
- As a visual reminder for brain-based teaching strategies, check out Chris Lema's "Sticky Teaching" graphic, which is on pages 164–169 and can also be downloaded at http://chrislema.com/wp-contentuploads/2012/05/StickyTeachingPoster.pdf.

MOVEMENT STRATEGIES

The benefits of movement in the classroom are undisputed and widely documented in the research. A very practical summary of research, along with many classroom activities, can be found in Eric Jensen's book *Learning With the Body in Mind: The Scientific Basis for Energizers, Movement, Play, Games and Physical Education* (2000a) and in my previous two books with Gurian and Stevens, *Strategies for Teaching Boys and Girls: Elementary Level* and *Strategies for Teaching Boys and Girls: Secondary Level* (2008). Movement comes in many forms in the classrooms. Sometimes, it comes in the form of an activity that the whole class does. Other times, movement is just for a few students who need it. There are even ways to provide outlets for movement for students who are sitting in their desks. Movement does not compete with instructional time—it enhances it. And for boys, especially, movement in the classroom is Mission Critical. If you don't provide it, they'll provide it for themselves (and not necessarily the kind you hope for).

> **Facts From Chris Lema's "Sticky Teaching" Poster**
>
> - 50% of our brain focuses on processing visual information.
> - We process visuals 6,000 times faster than text.
> - We forget 90% of what we learn in a month and most of it within an hour.
> - Getting the attention of students is critical. (Lema, 2012)

- There are several excellent ways to modify the classroom environment and class procedures to allow for movement, even while students are seated. For reminders about these strategies, please see Chapter 6.
- Provide active and less-active projects from which students can choose. I recall a second-grade classroom at Douglass Elementary in which a girls' reading group chose to create a large Venn diagram on the floor while the boys' reading group chose to do role-plays (acting out a battle scene, not surprisingly) as the characters from the book.

- Teach Brain Gym (2011) to students. These can be used by individual students, when they need it, while sitting at their desks. Brain Gym moves can also be used as all-class activities when you all need to take a stretch/movement break.
- Develop a list of movement-oriented activities that your whole class can do together when a learning break is needed. The ideas are endless and can be found with a quick search of "classroom movement" on the Internet. A new teacher-sharing website, http://www.teacherspayteachers.com, offers numerous packets of downloadable movement activities for an extremely nominal ($1–$6) charge. Some quick and easy examples include:
  - A one-minute "wiggle dance" to music in the primary classrooms;
  - Jumping jacks, hopping, or cherry-pickers;
  - Have a "snowball fight" with cotton balls or with slips of paper that have questions on them;
  - Turn on music and give instructions such as, "Walk around the room and touch five things that are plastic/glass/paper/cylindrical/machines";
  - High-five 10 people in the room;
  - Create a secret handshake with someone on the other side of the room; and
  - Play Rock-Paper-Scissors with three other people.
- Create learning activities that teach your content while getting students moving around. You will be amazed at how effectively these activities work for secondary students! A few examples include:
  - Play Simon Says to energize the classroom, as well as to review and assess. Include all sorts of movements, including cross-lateral activities (Brain Gym has good examples of these), sometimes while they are walking. Simon says, "Touch your toes if 6/9 is a reduced fraction" or "Using both hands and fingers, hold up a prime number between 30 and 40" (courtesy of teacher Chris Duhon).

- o Play silent ball from time to time during indoor recess or if they have earned a reward. Instead of just quietly throwing the ball, students have to call out a prime number before tossing the ball. They can use any prime number as long as they don't repeat one that has been said. You can do this with countries, states, and capitals, as well (courtesy of teacher Chris Duhon).
- o For movement in chemistry class, give students an element symbol. Have them determine the number of valence electrons found in that element. After they determine that information, they walk around the room to form either covalent or ionic bonds with another element. Once they pair up, they present themselves in front of the class, naming the compound correctly, as well as explaining the type of bond they formed and why (courtesy of teacher Jennifer Keil).
- o In Spanish class, have students stand up and ask someone three questions in Spanish. Have the other student respond—also in Spanish. Doing this every 15 minutes really reinforces whatever it is that you're working on and breaks up the instruction. It can be done in any content area and at any grade (courtesy of teacher Susan Hartman).
- Let students spend instructional time outdoors. In a study of children with attention deficit disorder, it was found that outdoor walks improved scores on tests of attention and concentration. Those who took walks in natural settings performed better than those who walked in urban areas. In fact, researchers found that a "dose of nature" worked as well as, or better than, a dose of medication in improving concentration (Berman, Jonides, & Kaplan, 2008).
- For books that provide more ideas for classroom movement, I recommend:
  - o Gurian, M., Stevens, K., & King, K. (2008a). *Strategies for Teaching Boys and Girls: Elementary Level* (PreK–5).
  - o Gurian, M., Stevens, K., & King, K. (2008b). *Strategies for Teaching Boys and Girls: Secondary Level* (Grades 6–12).

Researchers reported that participating in physical activity (including classroom-based physical activity) was positively related to outcomes including academic achievement, academic behaviors, and indicators of cognitive skills and attitudes, such as concentration, memory, self-esteem, and verbal skills.

Division of Adolescent and School Health, Centers for Disease Control and Prevention, July 2011.

- Summerford, C. (2005). *Action-Packed Classrooms: Movement Strategies to Invigorate K–5 Learners.*
- Jensen, E. (2000a). *Learning With the Body in Mind* (K–12).
- James, A., Allison, S., & McKenzie, C. (2010). *Active Lessons for Active Brains: Teaching Boys and Other Experiential Learners* (Grades 3–10).

WHAT DO EDUCATORS SAY ABOUT MOVEMENT?

I had a veteran teacher complain regarding the boys in her second-grade classroom who were unable to sit still during the phonics portion of the lesson. I suggested she let them stand. She incredulously asked, "I can do that?!?" I helped her process what would be needed to help this be a successful endeavor. We talked about expectations, parameters, and letting go of control. Within a week, she came back excited to tell me it was working!

Desha Bierbaum, principal, Wamsley Elementary School

In the classroom, boys are expected to sit for long periods of time, which leads to constant fidgeting, restlessness, inattentiveness, and agony for the poor girl sitting next to the boy. Movement should be part of every lesson plan.

Teacher of an all-boys 10th grade class

More than anything else, boys need constant switch-ups and involvement in their learning. Throughout a lesson, having turn-and-talks, teaching time, mirroring activities when learning a new strategy, and using body movement to learn something new will ensure that boys' attention spans are kept on the task at hand. It will also ensure that they are deeply integrating the new learning into their knowledge bank.

Stephanie Van Horn, fifth-grade teacher, Douglass Elementary School

STUDENT INTERESTS STRATEGIES

Research shows that students' interests are directly correlated to their achievement. (Caine & Caine, 1991; Schiefele & Csikszentmihalyi, 1995; Tomlinson, 1998). Tie in student interests as you teach the prescribed content—especially for boys who, with lower oxytocin levels,

If your school already demonstrates a strong commitment to keeping students active through classroom-based movement, physical education, and extracurriculars—or, if it is your goal to become an exemplar school—check out the Active Schools Acceleration Project, an initiative sponsored by Child Obesity 180. More information can be found at: http://www.childobesity180.org/our -initiatives/physical-activity/.

are less likely to do work in order to please others. First, administer an interest inventory to students to find out what they like to do at school, as well as *outside of school* (it's important to focus on outside-of-school interests because we want to bring the "real world" in!). There are a wide variety of student inventories, including interest inventories, online and available for free download. I like interest inventories that ask the kids about their interests in music, TV/movies, and hobbies. Once you know your students' interests, here are some examples of interest-based activities that teachers have shared with me:

- Math can be taught through topics that many boys will find fascinating. For many helpful examples, downloadable games, videos, and activity ideas, visit http://passyworldofmathematics.com/. This website has topics such as "Weight Training Math," "Off-Road Algebra," "AFL Football," "Tsunami Mathematics, "eBay Math," and much more. The site offers a free subscription.
- Learn the physics of amusement parks, battles and weapons, sports, and more at http://www.real-world -physics-problems.com/.
- For similar kinds of high-interest teaching resources, simply do an Internet search on the topic followed by

the words "lesson plan." For example, try "skateboarding lesson plan" or "hip-hop lesson plan."

- Use the lyrics of rock-and-roll music to teach poetry, as well as standards across the curriculum (see the Summer Teacher Institute lesson plans at http://www .rockhall.com).
- Teach technical reading and writing by having students create instruction manuals for things like fixing a car or playing a video game.
- Teach persuasive writing by having students write reviews for albums, movies, video games, or other popular media.
- When developing vocabulary or spelling lists, let boys pick a few words for the list that come from an area of interest.
- Create a PowerPoint slides how with pictures of students' interests. When they struggle with ideas of what to write, have them watch the slide show for inspiration.
- Start paying attention to students' pop culture. Get to know your young minds—what are they listening to, viewing, and playing?—even if you find it unappealing. Find ways to incorporate references and examples from pop culture into the lesson. Popular music is great for activity breaks and transitions, and it shows students that their interests are important in school.

TRY THIS

Take the teachers to the computer lab during a faculty meeting to do some Internet searching for high-interest and pop culture lessons that address the content standards. Have teachers create a shared document with the information shown below.

Subject Area	Content Standard/ Grade(s)	URL	Description of Site

REAL-WORLD LEARNING STRATEGIES

Boys need to know why they are being asked to learn things. "Everybody is motivated by challenge and solving problems, and we don't make use of that in schools enough," says Bruce Alberts, Professor Emeritus at the University of California, San Francisco, and former president of the National Academy of Sciences (Curtis & Bernard, 2011). Here are a just a few examples of how great teachers connect what they teach to the real world. (Note: Many of the examples in the "interests-based" section above fit into this category as well, and vice versa!):

- At King Middle School, in Portland, Maine, seventh-graders learn about soil bacteria through creating multi-media information pamphlets. They consult professional microbiologists and cartoonists, conduct original research, and then distribute their completed pamphlets to local garden centers, universities, and flower shops.
- At High Tech High, in San Diego, California, an 11th grade biology class uses DNA bar coding to develop forensic techniques that help protect African wildlife. The students share their findings with wildlife-protection officials.
- At Ferryway School, in Malden, Massachusetts, fifth-graders explore history, science, technology, and engineering by designing their own water wheels. By the time they visit the nearby Saugus Iron Works, a historic site that dates back to the 1640s, they've already tested and mastered the centuries-old technology.
- Have students plan and create a school garden plot along with school composting.
- Look for YouTube videos that show how the content is used in the real world and show experts in action.
- NASA.gov has many different teaching suggestions for math equations and ideas that are used to calculated space travel, time, and distance. Have students do a project that utilizes the information that can be found with NASA.

> Learning occurs when you apply it. It has to be hands-on. It has to be related. It can't be theoretical. How can we teach algebra to urban youth? We have to make it real and apply it.
>
> Leslie Block, PhD, consultant, Leslie S. Block & Associates

> The educational equivalent to real estate's "location, location, location" is "motivation, motivation, motivation."
>
> Melissa Kelly, secondary education blogger

- Use actual train and plane schedules to write story problems about speed, difference, time zones, and velocity.
- Do a parabola (or other shape) hunt. Find parabolas in real life, like the McDonald's arches, and analyze them. Find their dimensions and build equations around them.
- Have students write letters to real people about real issues that are important to them. This activity ties in well to studies of civics, government, and current events.
- Utilize simulations, such as those at http://www .teachinteract.com. Simulations are often competitive, as well as imitating real-world problems.
- Provide as many opportunities as possible for students to show their work to a wider audience. Creating products that only classmates and the teacher will see is not very motivating for a lot of students. With technology and a little planning, there is no reason that a student's audience should be so limited.
  - Have a student video-conference with a student at another school to share their work.
  - Have students post their work on your class website or on a wiki site.

> Let's try to appreciate boys for what they are. We need to widen the circle in our classrooms and make them boy friendlier by giving them more choice both in reading and in writing, more opportunities to collaborate, and a more active, kinetic atmosphere.
>
> Ralph Fletcher, author of *Guy Writer: What Guy Writers Need to Know* and *Boy Writers: Reclaiming Their Voices*

- o Have students create videos that can be posted to your class website or to a class YouTube account.
- o Have students share their work with older students from a neighboring middle or high school.

STUDENT CHOICE STRATEGIES

To be engaged as learners, students need to have some choice and control. Successful teachers help students develop the ability to make choices and give their students choices and control whenever possible (McCombs, 2012). Especially for boys who lack motivation or seem disengaged, it provides them with a sense of ownership and participation in their own learning. Students should have the opportunity to make decisions with the classroom every day. Here are a few ideas from teachers:

- A middle school teacher shares her unique choice board, which can be modified for any grade level or content area: "The choice board that I give to students looks like a menu from a restaurant. Students start off by picking one 'appetizer,' from the menu. There are three to four 'entrees' and students get to pick which one they want to do. In the 'a la carte' or 'side dish' section of the menu, I typically offer four choices, with students picking two of them. An optional enrichment activity is what we call 'dessert,' and kids can choose one for extra credit."
- There is a wonderful selection of downloadable choice boards at http://daretodifferentiate.wikispaces.com/Choice+Boards. As with anything nowadays, a quick Internet search yields many ideas and examples!
- During a unit of study, provide students with 2–3 novels from which to choose.
- During free reading, allow students to make choices within parameters. For example, some teachers use a "food pyramid" to allow 4–5 of a certain type of book and

only 1–2 of another type of book. A bingo card can also be distributed with boxes labeled "fiction," "nonfiction," "graphic novel," "comic book," "magazine," "at least 200 pages," and so on. Instruct students on how many and which types of boxes to guide their reading selections.

- Allow students to choose which type of software they use to create a report, such as Word, PowerPoint, or Publisher.
- Create Interest Centers that include a variety of learning activities to extend and reinforce the content—even at the secondary level!
- Give students more opportunities to write about topics of their own choosing, even if it means that students include more aggression themes (for a more thorough exploration of the topic of aggression themes in writing, see Chapter 4).
- Create many different options for books reports. Some examples include:
  - Create a slide show presentation to illustrate the major points of the chapter as if they were teachers teaching younger students.
  - Develop a newspaper article or a journalistic TV report about the chapter as if it were breaking news.
  - Prepare a debate on the chapter's main points and pose as either politicians or lawyers presenting their persuasive arguments.
  - Act out a scene about the contents of the chapter and perform it for the class.
  - Design a virtual field trip to study topics and concepts to be learned based on the content of the chapter.
- Give choice when it comes to homework too. Provide students with five homework options each week and have them choose three.
- Give assignments at the beginning of the week. For those who complete their assignments by Friday, there is no weekend homework. The others have the weekend to finish.

VISUAL-SPATIAL STRATEGIES

Boys—who, on average, have more cortical areas dedicated to visual-spatial processing—are especially drawn to visual input (Sax, 2005). Use boys' visual-spatial strengths to support their development in language and literacy areas with a few of these simple, yet highly effective, strategies.

- Have boys draw or storyboard their ideas prior to writing a story. These drawings serve as a form of graphic organizer or "non-linguistic representation" as Marzano, Pickering, & Pollock call it in their analysis of effective classroom practices (2001). For a fun introduction to storyboarding, there is a great YouTube video that shows the animators of *Toy Story* demonstrating their use of storyboards (search "Toy Story storyboards").

- Encourage more detail and color in pictures when you want the students' writing to have more detail and more adjectives. If your focus is on another trait of writing, such

Few boys are willing to slog through a novel if they know the reward is to answer a thousand questions, draw pretty postcards, and express how they felt about the characters/conflict/resolution. Whatever happened to reading a book just for enjoyment? Why do we feel compelled to make every event an assessment event? And if we must assess everything, do we always need a paper product to make that assessment authentic? Let's find ways to make reading fun, free of "work"-related assessments.

Eighth-grade teacher of an all-boys classroom

The unit is *Romeo and Juliet,* and the setting is Watts. Enthusiasm in the all-boys class is running high with all the bling and bang of inner-city rivalries. We acted out every sword fight that day. The paper towel tubes became a blur, and the words of the Bard rose over the sounds of the battle. It's 10 years later and I bump into a member of that class. What do you think he remembered from class?

Larry Hackett, educator and educational consultant

as ideas, organization, or voice, it may suffice for students to create simple pencil sketches before writing.

- Have students talk about their drawings with a partner before they start to write. This helps to "prime the pump" as students bridge from their visual to verbal constructs. Teachers at my school had students draw first, talk about their drawings with a partner next, then label their pictures with words, and start the process of writing after that.

- Allow students to create "on-topic" doodles and pictures while listening to a lecture. After 10–15 minutes of lecture, have students turn to a neighbor to share what they learned (and doodled or drew).

- For homework, have students illustrate what they learned in class with pictures and symbols only—no letters or words are allowed! The next day in class, have students exchange papers and try to label each other's illustrations with explanations.

- For any kind of class vocabulary or spelling, have students provide not only the definition but also an illustration (Olshansky, 2008).

- Have students illustrate class Word Walls.

- Take advantage of software programs such as KidPix, Kidspiration, and Inspiration, which create pictures and graphic organizers. Comic books are an appealing kind of graphic organizer, as well as story board. Find some free computer-based comic book creator tools at:
  - http://www.toondoo.com
  - http://www.stripcreator.com/make.php
  - http://www.makebeliefscomix.com/Comix/
  - http://www.comicmaster.org.uk

TECHNOLOGY STRATEGIES

The right classroom technology helps make learning more visual, more interactive, and more high interest. Increased productivity, quantity of work, quality of work, intrinsic motivation, and sense of empowerment have been documented in the research (Mouza, 2008). For students with more of a male orientation to their learning style—less eager to please, wanting visual and interactive content, and benefiting from more immediate feedback during the process—technology should be utilized to the fullest. The sky is really the limit here (and keeps changing); however, here are a few things to consider adding to your repertoire:

- Load MP3s with teacher- or student-created podcasts. These podcasts can be a review of prior lessons, or could be a student's report on a topic or a book report. These can be used to help students review old information, learn new information, or catch up on content if they missed school. Excellent high school podcast examples can be found on teacher Ben Boyer's biology website: http://schools.bvsd.org/p12/boulder/faculty/boyer/default.aspx.
- Promethean boards, interactive whiteboards specially designed for educational use, can be organized to contain folders with video links, music files, illustrations, and activity starters. They are visual and engaging and encourage active participation. If the cost of an interactive whiteboard is prohibitive, check out Johnny Lee's instructions on transforming any surface into an interactive board with the use of a $40 Wii remote. His solution provides 80% of the interactive board's functionality at about 1% of the cost: http://johnnylee.net/projects/wii/.
- Video-game development can be very motivating for many boys, while teaching creative problem solving, writing and storytelling skills, art and aesthetics, and 21st-century technology skills. Students develop video games, individually or collaboratively, that teach the content standards. Some schools, such as the East Austin College Prep charter school in Austin, Texas, require that students develop video games in the

content area where they are the weakest, based on assessment data. Students have the ability to interface with professional game developers worldwide and can enhance their technical writing skills through writing reviews, strategy manuals, and game instructions. A few sources include:

- o "Gamestar Mechanic" provides younger students with templates for creating games and offers a free basic level of service. It can be found at: http://gamestarmechanic.com/
- o World Wide Workshop and "Globaloria" develop applications for learning with technology that combine game mechanics and social networking for students ages 10 and up. Students learn to use more advanced Adobe Flash Player coding instead of templates: http://www.worldwideworkshop.org/.

- Create a few PowerPoint slide shows that contain pictures depicting students' interests. When students can't think of anything to write about, they can open the slide show for some ideas, or it can be projected and put in slide show mode during writing time. Pick action-packed and humorous pictures. Look on Pinterest for "writing picture prompts" to find some great ones shared by teachers.

- Wikis are online discussion boards where students can post book reviews, recommend books, and discover a great new book. Additionally, wikis provide a world-wide audience for boys' writing. This is invaluable for boys who need a little extra motivation to write:
  - o Set up your own class wiki here: http://www.wikispaces.com/content/teacher.
  - o Read and write book reviews on the Scholastic wiki: http://teacher.scholastic.com/activities/swyar/.

- Have students create "Book Trailers" as a book project. Like movie trailers, these book trailers are a fresh new take on regular old book reports. A helpful website with many examples of student-made book trailers, along with instructions on how to create your own, can be found at: http://www.booktrailersforreaders.com/.

- Use QR codes in the classroom. You know those black-and-white bar codes that are showing up everywhere? Well, they are popping up in classrooms. One middle school science class that I observed had students make digital recordings of oral reports about weather phenomena. Students then created a poster that illustrated the weather event and placed a QR code on the poster. Students with a smartphone or iPad with the free QR app could scan the QR code and listen to the audio report. More suggestions can be found for using QR codes in the classroom on various online teacher blogs.

COMPETITION STRATEGIES

Most boys love to compete, so why not use this natural desire to help you get the content across? Teach students that the fun of the competition is reward enough. Don't offer extra credit points or anything of value. Be specific about what "healthy competition" looks like (no put-downs, no yelling or arguing, etc.). The more your students struggle with good sportsmanship, the more important it is to teach and practice competition. Let students know that they need to be good sports in order to participate. As a supportive competitive environment

We need to help our boys be gracious winners and good losers. They can get very angry and worked up if they lose and braggadocios if they win. We encourage board games during inside recess and free time because they need to learn how to win and lose. Their natural way is to beat on their chest. We need to tone that down while recognizing that this is who they are.

Vermelle Greene, principal/founder (retired), SACRED Life Boys Academy

Boys love competition. Even though they are competing to see who is the top one, they are building the concept of "team" in the process because they help each other out.

ROTC Instructor

motivates boys, it helps girls build self-confidence (Shindler, 2009). To get your wheels turning, here are a just a few examples of how teachers incorporate games and competition in the classroom:

- Draw a football field on the board. Students get into teams and answer questions. Correct answers move the ball down the field to score a goal. Incorrect answers result in the loss of a down. Questions can be made more difficult (2-yard gain, or more difficult for a 30-yard gain). Students can decide if they want an easier question or if they want to go for the "Hail Mary."
- Fly Swatter Review: The answers to questions are written on the board. Each team has one fly swatter. When the teacher asks a question, the group confers and sends one runner to the board to swat the right answer. Teachers vary this by lining students up in two rows with the two students in the front holding the fly swatters. They compete to swat an answer, pass the swatter, and go to the back of the line.
- Marie, an elementary teacher, shares the following idea for Classroom Pictionary for review: "I break the class into teams of three and four students. I prepare five levels of notecards ahead of time. On each notecard I write single-word concepts or definitions. Level 1 cards are easiest, and Level 5 cards are very difficult. Each level card translates to equal point values. For example, a Level 3 card is worth three points. When the game begins, a team gets to pick a level card prior to viewing it. They must send one drawer up to the board. The drawer has 45 seconds to get their team to guess the word/concept on the card by drawing. The drawer cannot use numbers, letters, or symbols; if they do, the team's turn ends. If the team guesses correctly, they receive the point value. If they guess incorrectly, the card is passed to the next team, and an extra point is accumulated.

- Valerie, a high school teacher from Texas, shares: "For vocabulary review, I use the bean-bag toss. I divide the class into three groups, and they stay in their rows. The teams take turns, and the boys rotate. One boy throws the bean bag and when (if) he hits a target, he can answer the question to earn those points for his team. All the boys have their books open the whole time. They want to know the answer when it is someone else's turn! It's super easy for me. I borrow someone's note cards, shuffle them, and go in order so there are no accusations of 'stacking the deck.' And the boys like it because they get to stand up and throw stuff!"
- "Jeopardy," "Who Wants to be a Millionaire," and other game formats are both familiar and fun. Find many excellent downloadable and web-based tools (for free!) at http://superteachertools.com/.

SINGLE-GENDER GROUPING STRATEGIES

For coed schools, single-gender grouping can be another grouping strategy to add to your repertoire of grouping strategies (Gurian, Stevens & Daniels, 2009). Here are a few ways that single-gender grouping has worked effectively:

- Advisory classes are a great time for all-boys and all-girls groups. Single-gender advisories allow the group leader and students to address important social-emotional issues that may otherwise go unaddressed. For some ideas on supporting boys' journey to manhood during an all-boys advisory class, see the "mentoring" section of Chapter 5.
- Creating all-boy reading and novel study groups works for a few reasons. As a teacher, you can provide book options to an all-boy group that you wouldn't necessarily offer to a coed group because of lack of interest from girls. Also, boys' book discussions will likely differ from girls' in that they have the freedom to talk more about

the action sequences and less about the relational themes. Finally, if the students are to do a group project following the book, it can be easier for boys to come to agreement about what kind of project to do.

- An all-boys writing class is a not-to-be-missed opportunity. Start by separating students by gender for just one writing unit—perhaps 3–4 weeks in length. You will notice that boys' enthusiasm for writing goes up when they have the opportunity to write with and for other boys. Add in some grammar competitions, relax your rules on aggression themes, and laugh with them when they write about farts and boogers. Students will soon be asking for their "gender groups" again. In grades 2–6, be sure to use Ralph Fletcher's *Guy Write* (2011) as a read-aloud. If you are a teacher of boy writers, here are some more books that I highly recommend:

  o For the K–8 teacher: *Boy Writers: Reclaiming Their Voices* (2006) by Ralph Fletcher.

  o For the K–8 teacher: *Me Read? No Way! A Practical Guide to Improving Boys' Literacy Skills* by the Ontario Provincial Government.

  o For the Grade 6–12 teacher: *Reading Don't Fix No Chevys: Literacy in the Lives of Young Men* (2002) by Michael Smith and Jeffrey Wilhelm.

  o For the Grade 6–12 teacher: *Going With the Flow: How to Engage Boys (and Girls) in Their Literacy Learning* (2006) by Michael Smith and Jeffrey Wilhelm.

  o For the Grade 3–8 student: *Guy-Write: What Every Guy Writer Needs to Know* by Ralph Fletcher.

- Offer a Boys Writing Club as an extracurricular activity, with a focus on writing for fun. Ben Tilley, principal of Ridgeway Elementary School in Missouri, does just that. Boys meet once a week during lunch and get free choice of what to write about—very little is considered out of bounds. They can move around to work where they like. If they start to get off task, the group has a code word (a really disgusting "secret" word that they all agreed on) that cues students to get back to work.

MUSIC STRATEGIES

Music has many benefits, including activating the brain, creating emotion, reducing stress, improving memory, and aiding mental processing (E. Jensen, 2000b).

Gender-based writing and reading groups appear to have a big impact. We also embraced the use of graphic novels for boys and letting boys write about things they are interested in. It helped the teachers in our building to step back and reassess what they value in boys' writing.

Mike Keppler, principal, Niwot Elementary School

- Using background music (including environmental sounds) can promote learning if it is used approximately 10–30% of the time and is predictable so that it does not distract (E. Jensen, 2000b). Music without lyrics works especially well in the classroom.
- Some teachers use music effectively to cue transitions in the room, such as when it is time to rotate to a different station or time to clean up. A high school biology teacher shared with me that she plays "Should I Stay or Should I Go Now?" by The Clash to get her students to clean up before the bell rings. I've observed a second-grade teacher use calm, classical music to cue students to make a transition.
- Set up playlists of music on an MP3 player or on your computer. Connect to amplification and consider purchasing a remote so that it is easy to select and play music from anywhere in the classroom.
- For excellent research and practical suggestions for using music in the classroom, I recommend the following books by Eric Jensen:
  - *Music With the Brain in Mind* (2000b)
  - *Arts With the Brain in Mind* (2001)
- Excellent web resources for incorporating music in the classroom include:
  - More research and music suggestions from Eric Jensen: http://www.jensenlearning.com/news/the-perfect-music-for-brain-based-learning/brain-based-learning (2011)

- o Brain-friendly classroom music CDs: http://www
  .kaganonline.com/catalog/music.php
- o Teacher lesson plans that incorporate rock music
  into all areas of the curriculum: http://rockhall
  .com/education/inside-the-classroom/summer
  -teacher-institute/STI-lesson-plans/
- o Lesson plans for teaching the curriculum through
  rap music: http://www.educationalrap.com
- o Teaching suggestions, lyrics, and music of all genres
  for all content areas: http://www.songsforteaching
  .com and http://www.songsthatteach.com
- Worried about young people's taste in music? Here are
  some "safe" and popular music recommendations:
  - o Flo Rida's "Good Feeling"
  - o OutKast's "Hey Ya!"
  - o Rihanna featuring Calvin Harris's "We Found Love"
  - o Pitbull's "Back in Time"
  - o David Guetta featuring Usher's "Without You"
  - o Taio Cruz's "Dynamite"
  - o Flo Rida featuring David Guetta's "Club Can't
    Handle Me"
  - o Bruno Mars's "It Will Rain"

TEST PREPARATION STRATEGIES

Executive functioning in the brain is what helps us to plan, organize, pay attention, remember details, and manage our time. Executive functioning also helps us to delay gratification. Since maturation of the part of the brain responsible for executive functioning occurs later in boys (Lenroot et al., 2007), boys will likely struggle more than girls in the areas of study habits and test

> The beauty of education today is that so much of what students can do today is self-directed. Sitting and listening to someone drone on is not engaging. There is no reason to do that nowadays.
>
> Brewster Ely, headmaster, Town School for Boys

preparation skills. Teach boys a variety of specific methods for preparing; otherwise, for some boys, their efforts will be disorganized and fleeting. Boys need specificity around exactly what they should do, by when, and how they should do it.

- Give students the option to create one 3" × 5" study card that they can fill with information (both sides) and use during the test. Just the act of filling the card with important information goes a long way toward learning the content.
- Brainstorm a list of ways that students can demonstrate their learning, including assessments that are not paper and pencil. Give students some choice on one part of an assessment.
- For a homework assignment one night, have students create problems or questions for the test. Use some of these problems on the actual test.
- Provide students with a practice copy of the test in advance. Make sure that it uses the same format as the actual test (short-answer, multiple choice, etc.) and make sure it covers the same general content (for example, in math, it gives the same kinds of problems with different numbers).
- There are a variety of test-taking and study tips available at: http://testtakingtips.com/ and http://studygs .net/. Depending on the age of your students, these sites would be for your reference and/or student reference. Don't neglect this important area of teaching, especially for boys who may not come by this naturally!

TEST ADMINISTRATION STRATEGIES

An undeniable part of the teaching and learning process is the assessment phase. With all of your hard work to address the learning styles of your students, you want to also ensure that the testing environment is optimal. Here are a number of tips that you may be able to incorporate. For assessments with strict proctoring guidelines, be sure to check what is allowed and what is not allowed:

- Peppermint odor has been shown to increase alertness in the brain (Barker et al., 2003).
- Chewing gum has been shown to increase test scores, both as a result of the insulin receptors in the brain and as a result of the rhythmic chewing motion of the jaw (Onyper, 2011).
- Give students access to drinking water during testing. It helps reduce stress hormones in the bloodstream (Ganio et al., 2011).
- Give students affirming messages before they take the test. The "stereotype threat," which was discussed in Chapter 4, is a well-documented phenomenon that depresses students' performance on tests (Hartley et al. 2010).
- If it is necessary for students to indicate their sex on the form, have them complete this section after they finish the test, not before.
- Allow students to talk about and/or write about test anxiety before taking high-stakes tests. For both males and females, this has been shown to improve test scores (E. Jensen, 2008).
- It is helpful for students to go on a walk before sitting for a test. It helps decrease stress while increasing blood flow and oxygen to the brain. Have students pair up and discuss what will be on the test as they walk (Luciana, Collins, & Depue, 1998).
- It is preferable if students can have their test proctored in the same location where they learned the content and by the same teacher for that content area (Schwabe & Wolf, 2009).
- Some studies indicate that students may perform better in single-gender testing environments with same-gender teachers, especially for boys in literacy and girls in math (APA, 2006). If you decide to re-arrange

students in this way, have them also practice/prepare for the test in this arrangement so that they are familiar with their surroundings on test day. If you just make these changes on test day, research shows that it will hurt more than help!

THE FINAL BUZZER

This chapter helps teachers transform their classroom practice to energize and engage their male learners as well as their female learners. Use this chapter as a coaching and planning tool during professional development, teacher coaching, professional goal setting, and even student support (Response to Intervention) meetings.

- Anticipate teachers' concerns about boy-friendly classroom strategies early and allow opportunities to acknowledge and process these issues.
- Boys' perceptions of school and of learning are formed in the classroom. Every single classroom and every single staff member must be on board.
- At the same time, not every teacher needs to be implementing the same strategies in the same way. Allow instructors to identify what they are already doing and what new strategies should be prioritized for implementation in their settings. Engage teachers in discussions about their implementation plans throughout the school year during coaching and evaluation conferences.
- The vast majority of these strategies don't require more time or more money. They require an understanding of boys' brain-based learning needs and an openness on the part of all educators to re-thinking traditional teaching methods. Seize opportunities to substitute active for sedentary; interactive for solitary; relevant for irrelevant; multisensory for auditory only; laughter for apathy.

But the dream is never forgotten, only put aside and never out of reach: Where once the dream connected boys with the world of men, now it reconnects men with the spirit of boys.

John Thorn, Major League Baseball historian

Additional materials and resources related to *Writing the Playbook: A Practitioner's Guide to Creating a Boy-Friendly School* can be found at www.boyfriendlyschools.com. Kelley King can be reached at kelleykingpd@hotmail.com.

Afterword

I was compelled to write this book because classroom teachers cannot do this work alone. In every school, we can find individual classrooms that are amazingly boy friendly. That is wonderful—but it is not enough. We need entire schools to make a comprehensive and broad-based commitment to better understanding the developmental and educational needs of boys. That takes leadership. Leaders need leadership strategies—and that is where this book comes in.

Boy-friendly schools need principals and teacher leaders who are informed about the brain research, who can get people charged up, and who are bold enough to rewrite or throw away short-sighted policies. Boy-friendly schools need leaders who will encourage and support teachers as they change the way they teach. They need leaders who are committed to both boys and girls, and who realize that this is not a zero-sum game. Boys need adults who genuinely like them.

Wherever you are in the process of addressing the needs of boys and closing gaps, I hope that this book can serve as a support system and a guide in taking the next steps to creating a school where boys can truly thrive; a school that celebrates boys; a school where boys can be boys.

Sticky Teaching Graphic

Chris Lema

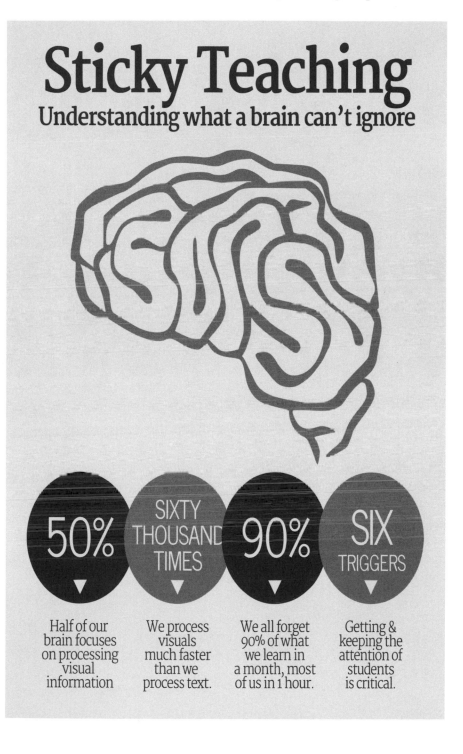

Sticky Teaching
Understanding what a brain can't ignore

50%
▼
Half of our brain focuses on processing visual information

SIXTY THOUSAND TIMES
▼
We process visuals much faster than we process text.

90%
▼
We all forget 90% of what we learn in a month, most of us in 1 hour.

SIX TRIGGERS
▼
Getting & keeping the attention of students is critical.

The ABC's of
Sticky Teaching

A Awaken the Intrigue

B Begin & End often

C Create lots of Contrast

D Draw them in w/ Stories

E Emotion drives Attention

F Focus on the Big Idea

Why do these work?

Interrupts (starts & stops) make the brain check in.

The reptilian brain checks to see if there's any danger. When it discovers you're boring, it checks out again.

The brain is wired for authentic stories.

The brain is constantly trying to save your life. So everything else is competing with it. Stories build trust, which enables the brain to take a break.

The brain doesn't need unnecessary details.

When data is stored in the brain, only the "main thing" gets stored. Like reading headlines. So stick with the big idea and repeat it often.

Teach unpredictably, but don't quit the routines.

Predictability reduces stress in the brain which helps it recover from other stress. Combined with repetition, it helps encode information faster. So use the clock & timings to your advantage.

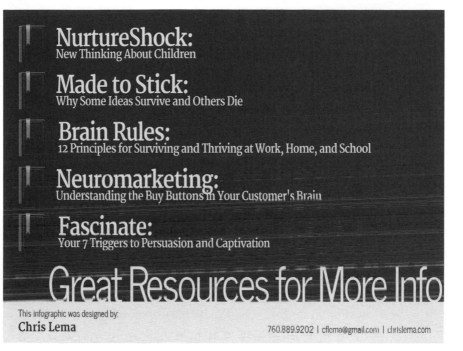

NurtureShock:
New Thinking About Children

Made to Stick:
Why Some Ideas Survive and Others Die

Brain Rules:
12 Principles for Surviving and Thriving at Work, Home, and School

Neuromarketing:
Understanding the Buy Buttons in Your Customer's Brain

Fascinate:
Your 7 Triggers to Persuasion and Captivation

Great Resources for More Info

This infographic was designed by:
Chris Lema

760.889.9202 | cflcma@gmail.com | chrislema.com

Source: Copyright by Chris Lema. Reprinted with permission.

References

Alivisatos, B., & Petrides, M. (1997, December 16). Functional activation of the human brain during mental rotation. *Neuropsychologia, 35*(2), 111–118.

American College of Sports Medicine. (2010). *Exercise is good medicine for preventing and reducing an angry mood.* Retrieved from ACSM in the News: http://www.acsm.org/about-acsm/media-room/ acsm-in-the-news/2011/08/01/exercise-is-good-medicine-for -preventing-and-reducing-an-angry-mood

American Psychological Association (APA). (2006, July 15). *Stereotype threat widens achievement gap.* Retrieved from American Psychological Association: http://www.apa.org/research/ action/stereotype.aspx

Andrade, J. (2010, January). What does doodling do? *Applied Cognitive Psychology,* 100–106.

Barker, S., Grayhem, P., Koon, J., Perkins, J., Whalen, A., & Raudenbush, B. (2003, December). Improved performance on clerical tasks associated with administration of peppermint odor. *Perceptual Motor Skills, 97*(3 Pt. 1), 1007–1010.

Baron-Cohen, S. (2002, June). The extreme male brain theory of autism. *Trends in Cognitive Science, 6*(6), 248–254.

Baron-Cohen, S. (2004). *The essential difference: Male and female brains and the truth about autism.* New York, NY: Perseus Books.

Barros, R., Silver, E., & Stein, R. (2009, February 1). School recess and group classroom behavior. *Pediatrics: Official Journal of the American Academy of Pediatrics, 123*(2), 431–436. Retrieved from: http:// pediatrics.aappublications.org/content/123/2/431.full.html

Batmanghelidj, F. (1997). *Your body's many cries for water: You are not sick, you are thirsty.* Falls Church, VA: Global Health Solutions, Inc.

Bechtel, L. (2004). *Doing morning meeting: The essential components.* Retrieved from Stenhouse Publishers: http://www.stenhouse.com/pdfs/0386guid.pdf

Bennett, C. M., & Baird, A. A. (2006, September). Anatomical changes in the emerging adult brain: A voxel-based morphometry study. *Human Brain Mapping, 27*, 766–777.

Berman, M. G., Jonides, J., & Kaplan, S. (2008, December). The cognitive benefits of interacting with nature. *Psychological Science, 19*(12), 1207–1212.

Bertrand, M., & Pan, J. (2011, October). *The trouble with boys: Social influences and the gender gap in disruptive behavior.* Retrieved from National Bureau of Educational Research: http://papers.nber.org/papers/w17541

Blundin, P. (2010). *Education gender issues: Do boys and girls really learn differently?* Retrieved from EduGuide: http://www.eduguide.org/library/viewarticle/33

Boorman, P. (2008, March/April). School culture, school climate: They are not the same thing. *Principal, 87*(4), 56–59.

Brain Gym International/Educational Kinesiology Foundation. (2011). *Home.* Retrieved from Brain Gym International: http://braingym.org/

Brizendine, L. (2008). *The female brain.* New York, NY: Random House.

Brizendine, L. (2010). *The male brain.* New York, NY: Random House.

Brooks, R. (2000, September). Robert Brooks PhD. Retrieved from Education and "Charismatic" Adults: http://www.drrobertbrooks.com/writings/articles/0009.html

Bunce, D. M., Flens, E. A., & Neiles, K. Y. (2010). How long can students pay attention in class? A study of student attention decline using clickers. *Journal of Chemical Education, 87*, 1438–1443.

Cahill, L. (2005). *His brain, her brain.* Retrieved from *Scientific American:* http://www.scientificamerican.com/article.cfm?id=his-brain-her-brain

Cain, J., Anderson, M., Cavert, C., & Heck, T. (2010). *Teambuilding puzzles: 100 puzzles and activities for creating teachable moments in creative problem solving, consensus building, leadership, exploring diversity, group decision making, goal setting, active learning, communication & teamwork.* Dubuque, IA: Kendall Hunt Publishing.

Cain, J., Cummings, M., & Stanchfield, J. (2012). *A teachable moment: A facilitator's guide to activities for processing, debriefing, reviewing, and reflection.* Dubuque, IA: Kendall Hunt Publishing.

Cain, J., & Jolliff, B. (2010). *Teamwork and teamplay: A guide to cooperative, challenge, and adventure activities that build confidence, cooperation, teamwork, creativity, trust, decision making, conflict resolution, resource management, communication, and effective feedback.* Dubuque, IA: Kendall Hunt Publishing.

Caine, R. N., & Caine, G. (1991). *Making connections: Teaching and the human brain.* Alexandria, VA: Association for Supervision and Curriculum Development.

Cannon, C. (2010). *Winning back our boys: The ultimate game plan for parents & teachers.* Scottsdale, AZ: LifeSuccess Publishing.

CBS (Director). (2001). *The delinquents* [Motion picture]. Available for purchase at: http://gurianinstitute.com/products/products-for-educators/

Center on Education Policy. (2010). *Are there differences in achievement between boys and girls?* Washington, DC: Author.

Center on Education Policy. (2012). *Can goals motivate students?* Retrieved from http://www.cep-dc.org/cfcontent_file.cfm?Attachment=UsherKober_Background3_Motivation_5.22.12.pdf

Centers for Disease Control and Prevention (CDC). (2012, November 16). *Morbidity and Mortality Weekly Report (MMWR).* Retrieved from CDC Home: http://www.cdc.gov/nchs/nhis.htm

Chaplin, D., & Klasik, D. (2006). *Gender gaps in college and high school graduation by race, combining public and private schools.* Washington, DC: Urban Institute.

ChildObesity180. (n.d.). *The Active Schools Acceleration Project (ASAP).* Retrieved from ChildObesity180: http://www.childobesity180.org/our-initiatives/physical-activity/

Ciani, K. D., & Sheldon, K. M. (2010, March). *A versus F:* The effects of implicit letter priming on cognitive performance. *The British Journal of Educational Psychology, 80*(Pt. 1), 99–119.

Crisis. (n.d.). In *Merriam-Webster.com.* Retrieved from http://www.merriam-webster.com/dictionary/crisis

Curtis, D., & Bernard, S. (2011, July 27). *Project-based learning: Real-world issues motivate students.* Retrieved from Edutopia: http://www.edutopia.org/project-based-learning-student-motivation

Deak, J., & Ackerley, S. (2010). *Your fantastic, elastic brain: Stretch it, shape it.* Belvedere, CA: Little Pickle Press.

Division of Adolescent and School Health, National Center for Chronic Disease Prevention and Health Promotion. (2011,

September 16). School health guidelines to promote healthy eating and physical activity. Retrieved from Centers for Disease Control and Prevention: http://www.cdc.gov/mmwr/preview/mmwrhtml/rr6005a1.htm?s_cid=rr6005a1_x

Draganski, B., Gaser, C., Busch, V., Schuierer, G., Bogdahn, U., & May, A. (2004, January 22). Neuroplasticity: Changes in grey matter induced by training. *Nature, 427,* 311–312.

Draves, W., & Coates, J. (2006). *Smart boys bad grades: Why boys get worse grades and are only 35% of graduates in higher education.* Retrieved from Smart Boys Bad Grades: http://www.smart boysbadgrades.com/smartboys_badgrades.pdf

Edwards, L., & Torcellini, P. (2002, July). *A literature review of the effects of natural light on building occupants.* Retrieved from Natural Renewable Energy Laboratory: http://www.nrel.gov/docs/fy02osti/30769.pdf

Fletcher, R. (2006). *Boy writers: Reclaiming their voices.* Portland, ME: Stenhouse Publishers.

Fletcher, R. (2012). *Guy-write: What every guy writer needs to know.* New York, NY: Henry Holt and Company.

Ganio, M., Armstrong, L., Casa, D., McDermott, B., Lee, E., Yamamoto, L., . . . Lieberman, H. (2011). Mild dehydration impairs cognitive performance and mood of men. *British Journal of Nutrition, 106,* 1535–1543.

Gershoff, E. T. (2002). Corporal punishment by parents and associated child behaviors and experiences: A meta-analytic and theoretical review. *Psychological Bulletin, 128,* 539–579

Giedd, J. (n.d.). Inside the teenage brain. (Frontline, Interviewer). Retrieved from http://www.pbs.org/wgbh/pages/frontline/shows/teenbrain/interviews/giedd.html

Giedd, J. N. (2004). Structural magnetic resonance imaging of the adolescent brain. *Annals of New York Academy of Sciences, 1021,* 77–85.

Giedd, J. N., Blumenthal, J., Jeffries, N. O., Castellanos, F. X., Liu, H., Zijdenbos, A., . . . Rappaport, J. L. (1999, October). Brain development during childhood and adolescence: A longitudinal MRI study. *Nature Neuroscience, 2*(10). Retrieved from Tel Aviv University, School of Mathematical Sciences: http://www.math.tau.ac.il/~dms/Longitudinal/brain_MRI.pdf

Goleman, D. (2006). *Emotional intelligence: Why it can matter more than IQ.* New York, NY: Random House.

Greene, J., & Winters, M. (2006). *Leaving boys behind: Public high school graduation rates.* New York, NY: Manhattan Institute for Policy Research.

Gruenert, S. (2008, March/April). School culture, school climate: They are not the same. *Principal.* Retrieved from http://www.naesp.org/resources/2/Principal/2008/M-Ap56.pdf

Guiso, L., Monte, F., Sapienza, P., & Zinglaes, L. (2008, May 30). Culture, math, and gender. *Science, 320*(5880), 1164–1165.

Gurian, M. (1997). *The wonder of boys.* New York, NY: Putnam.

Gurian, M. (1999). *A fine young man: What parents, mentors, and educators can do to shape adolescent boys into exceptional men.* New York, NY: Penguin Putnam.

Gurian, M. (2010). *The purpose of boys: Helping our sons find meaning, significance, and direction in their lives.* San Francisco, CA: Jossey-Bass.

Gurian, M., & Annis, B. (2008). *Leadership and the sexes: Using gender science to create success in business.* San Francisco, CA: Jossey-Bass.

Gurian, M., & Stevens, K. (2004, November). With boys and girls in mind. *Educational Leadership, 62*(3), 21–26.

Gurian, M., & Stevens, K. (2005). *The minds of boys: Saving our sons from falling behind in school and life.* San Francisco, CA: Jossey-Bass.

Gurian, M., & Stevens, K. (2010). *Boys and girls learn differently! A guide for teachers and parents.* San Francisco, CA: Jossey-Bass.

Gurian, M., Stevens, K., & Daniels, P. (2009). *Successful single-sex classrooms: A practical guide to teaching boys and girls separately.* San Francisco, CA: Jossey-Bass.

Gurian, M., Stevens, K., & King, K. (2008a). *Strategies for teaching boys and girls: Elementary level.* San Francisco, CA: Jossey-Bass.

Gurian, M., Stevens, K., & King, K. (2008b). *Strategies for teaching boys and girls: Secondary level.* San Francisco, CA: Jossey-Bass.

Haier, R., Karama, S., Leyba, L., & Jung, R. E. (2009). MRI assessment of cortical thickness and functional activity changes in adolescent girls following three months of practice on a visual-spatial task. *BMC Research Notes, 2,* 174.

Hanlon, H. W., Thatcher, R. W., & Cline, M. J. (1999). Gender differences in the development of EEG coherence in normal children. *Developmental Neuropsychology, 16*(3), 479–506.

Hartley, B., & Sutton, R. (2010). Children's development of stereo-typical gender-related expectations about academic engagement and consequences for performance. Poster presented at the British Educational Research Association (BERA) Annual Conference, University of Warwick, September 1–4.

Herlitz, A., & Rehnman, J. (2008). Sex differences in episodic memory. *Current Directions in Psychological Science, 17*(1), 52–56.

Hines, M. (2006). Prenatal testosterone and gender-related behaviour. *European Journal of Endocrinology, 155,* S115–S121.

Holcomb, E. L. (1999). *Getting excited about data: How to combine people, passion, and proof.* Thousand Oaks, CA: Corwin.

Horseman, N. D. (2006, June 13). Letter to the editor. *New York Times.* Retrieved from http://www.nytimes.com

Howe, A. C. (1996, December 9). Adolescents' motivation, behavior and achievement in science. Retrieved from National Association for Research in Science Teaching: http://www.narst.org/publications/research/Adolescent.cfm

Institute of Education Sciences. (2008, September). Office for Civil Rights survey redesign: A feasibility survey. Retrieved from National Center for Education Statistics: http://nces.ed.gov/surveys/frss/publications/92130/index.asp?sectionid=3

Jacket, M. (2010, March). Independent School District 196. Retrieved from *Occupational Therapy Newsletter,* Vol. 9: http://www.district196.org/or/Site%20PDFS/OT%20News%20Letter/9th%20School%20Tools.pdf

James, A. (2007). *Teaching the male brain: How boys think, feel, and learn in school.* Thousand Oaks, CA: Corwin.

James, A., Allison, S., & McKenzie, C. (2010). *Active lessons for active brains: Teaching boys and other experiential learners.* Thousand Oaks, CA: Corwin.

Jensen, E. (1998). *Teaching with the brain in mind.* Alexandria, VA: Association of Supervision and Curriculum Development.

Jensen, E. (2000a). *Learning with the body in mind: The scientific basis for energizers, movement, play, games, and physical education.* San Diego, CA: The Brain Store.

Jensen, E. (2000b). *Music with the brain in mind.* Thousand Oaks, CA: Corwin.

Jensen, E. (2001). *Arts with the brain in mind.* Alexandria, VA: Association of Supervision and Curriculum Development.

Jensen, E. (2005). *Top tunes for teaching: 977 song titles & practical tools for choosing the right music every time.* San Francisco, CA: Corwin.

Jensen, E. (2008, February). A fresh look at brain-based education. *Phi Delta Kappan, 89*(6), 408–417.

Jensen, E. (2009). *Teaching with poverty in mind: What being poor does to kids' brains and what schools can do about it.* Alexandria, VA: Association of Supervision and Curriculum Development.

Jensen, E. (2011, February 27). *The perfect music for brain-based learning.* Retrieved from Jensen Learning: http://www.jensenlearning.com/news/the-perfect-music-for-brain-based-learning/brain-based-learning

Jensen, P. S., Mrazek, D., Knapp, P. K., Steinberg, L., Pfeffer, C., Schowalter, J., et al. (1997). Evolution and revolution in child psychiatry: ADHD as a disorder of adaptation. *Journal of the American Academy of Child and Adolescent Psychiatry, 36*(12), 1672–1681.

Katch, J. (2001). *Under deadman's skin: Discovering the meaning of children's violent play.* Boston, MA: Beacon Press.

Kindlon, D., & Thompson, M. (1999). *Raising Cain: Protecting the emotional life of boys.* New York, NY: Ballantine Books.

King, M. (1999). *Measurement of differences in emotional intelligence of preservice educational leadership students and practicing administrators as measured by the multifactor emotional intelligence scale.* Dissertation Abstracts International, *60*(3), 606.

King, K., & Gurian, M. (2006, September). Teaching to the minds of boys. *Educational Leadership, 64*(1), 56–61.

King, K., Gurian, M., & Stevens, K. (2010, November). Gender-friendly schools. *Educational Leadership, 68*(3), 38–42.

Kleinfeld, J. (2009, June). The state of American boyhood. *Gender Issues, 26*(2), 113–129.

Knez, I. (1995, March). Effects of indoor lighting on mood and cognition. *Journal of Environmental Psychology, 15*(1), 39–51.

Kuo, F., & Taylor, A. (2004). A potential natural treatment for attention-deficit/hyperactivity disorder: Evidence from a national study. Retrieved from *American Journal of Public Health, 94*(9), 1580–1586.

Lee, C. E., & Owens, R. G. (2003). *The psychology of men's health.* Buckingham, UK: Open University Press.

Lee, J., & Harley, V. R. (2012, June). The male fight-flight response: A result of SRY regulation of catecholamines? *BioEssays, 34*(6), 454–457.

Lema, C. (2012). Sticky teaching. Retrieved from Chris Lema: http://chrislema.com/wp-content/uploads/2012/05/StickyTeachingPoster.pdf

Lenroot, R., Gogtay, N., Greenstein, D., Wells, E., Wallace, G., Clasen, L., . . . Giedd, J. (2007). Sexual dimorphism of brain developmental trajectories during childhood and adolescence. *NeuroImage, 36,* 1065–1073.

Losen, D., & Orfield, G. (2002). *Racial inequality in special education.* Cambridge, MA: Harvard Education Press.

Luciana, M., Collins, P. F., & Depue, R. A. (1998). Opposing roles for dopamine and serotonin in the modulation of human spatial working memory functions. *Cerebral Cortex, 8*(3), 218–226.

Luscombe, B. (2010). Workplace salaries: At last, women on top. Retrieved from *Time*: http://www.time.com/time/business/article/0,8599,2015274,00.html

Mandal, A. (2012, December 10). Dopamine functions. Retrieved from *Medical News:* http://www.news-medical.net/health/Dopamine-Functions.aspx

Marzano, R., Pickering, D., & Pollock, J. (2001). *Classroom instruction that works.* Alexandria, VA. Association of Supervision and Curriculum Development.

McCombs, B. (2012). Developing responsible and autonomous learners: A key to motivating students. Retrieved from American Psychological Association: http://www.apa.org/education/k12/learners.aspx?item=7

Miller, B. C. (2004). *Quick team-building activities for busy managers: 50 exercises that get results in just 15 minutes.* New York, NY: AMACOM Books.

Miller, B. C. (2008). *50 quick meeting openers for busy managers.* New York, NY: AMACOM Books.

Moloney, J. (2002). *Ideas for getting boys into reading.* Retrieved from http://www.jamesmoloney.com.au/Ideas_for_Getting_Boys_into_Reading.htm

Montgomery, G. (2012). *Color blindness: More prevalent among males.* Retrieved from Howard Hughes Medical Institute: http://www.hhmi.org/senses/b130.html

Mouza, C. (2008). Learning with laptops: Implementation and outcomes in an urban, under-privileged school. *Journal of Research on Technology in Education, 40*(4), 447–473.

National Center for Educational Statistics. (2005). *National Assessment of Educational Progress (NAEP).* Retrieved from National Center for Educational Statistics: http://nces.ed.gov/nationsreportcard/reading/

National Institute of Building Sciences. (2012). *Home.* Retrieved from National Clearinghouse for Educational Facilities: http://www.ncef.org/

Noguera, P. (2008). *The trouble with black boys and other reflections on race, equity, and the future of public education*. San Francisco, CA: Wiley & Sons.

O'Connor, K. (2010). *A repair kit for grading: 15 fixes for broken grades* (2nd ed.). Portland, OR: Educational Testing Service.

Olshansky, B. (2008). *The power of pictures: Creating pathways to literacy through art*. San Francisco, CA: Jossey-Bass.

Ontario Ministry of Education. (2004). *Me read? No way! A practical guide to improving boys' literacy skills*. Retrieved from Ontario Ministry of Education: http://www.edu.gov.on.ca/eng/document/brochure/meread/meread.pdf

Ontario Ministry of Education. (2009). *Me read? And how! Ontario teachers report on how to improve boys' literacy skills*. Retrieved from Ontario Ministry of Education: http://www.edu.gov.on.ca/eng/curriculum/meRead_andHow.pdf

Onyper, S. (2011, October). Cognitive advantages of chewing gum. *Appetite, 57*(2), 321–328.

Organisation for Economic Co-operation and Development. (n.d.). Centre for Educational Research and Innovation (CERI)—Brain and Learning. Retrieved from OECD: http://www.oecd.org/document/63/0,3746,en_21571361_49995565_38792447_1_1_1_1,00.html

Payne, R., & Slocumb, P. (2011). *Boys in poverty: A framework for understanding dropout*. Bloomington, IN: Solution Tree Press.

PBS Parents. (n.d.a). *Understanding and raising boys: Logical solutions*. Retrieved from http://www.pbs.org/parents/raisingboys/school05.html

PBS Parents. (n.d.b). *Understanding and raising boys: Many ways to be a man*. Retrieved from http://www.pbs.org/parents/raisingboys/masculinity05.html

Planty, N., Provasnik, S., Hussar, W., Snyder, T., Kena, G., Hampden-Thompson, G., . . . Choy, S. (2007). *Condition of Education 2007*. Washington, DC: National Center for Education Statistics.

Rappaport, M., Bolden, J., Sarver, D., & Alderson, J. (2009). Hyperactivity in boys with attention-deficit/hyperactivity disorder (ADHD): A ubiquitous core symptom or manifestation of working memory deficits? *Journal of Abnormal Child Psychology, 37*(4), 521–534.

Ready, D., LoGerfo, L., Burkham, D., & Lee, V. (2005). Explaining girls' advantage in kindergarten literacy learning: Do classroom behaviors make a difference? *The Elementary School Journal, 106*(1), 21–38.

Richter, W., Ugurbil, K., Georgopoulos, A., & Kim, S.-G. (1997). Time-resolved fMRI of mental rotation. *NeuroReport, 8*, 3697–3702.

Roberts, A. (2001). *Safe teen: Powerful alternatives to violence.* Vancouver, Canada: Polestar.

Ruttle, P., Shirtcliff, E., Serbin, L., Fisher, D., Stack, D., & Schwartzman, A. (2011, January). Disentangling psychobiological mechanisms underlying internalizing and externalizing behaviors in youth: Longitudinal and concurrent associations with cortisol. *Hormones and Behavior, 59*(1), 123–132.

Ryff, C. D., Singer, B. H., Wing, E., & Love, G. D. (2001). Elective affinities and uninvited agonies: Mapping emotions with significant others onto health. In C. D. Ryff & B. H. Singer (Eds.), *Emotion, social relationships, and health* (pp. 133–174). New York, NY: Oxford University Press.

Sax, L. (2005). *Why gender matters: What parents and teachers need to know about the emerging science of sex differences.* New York, NY: Doubleday.

Sax, L. (2006). *Why gender matters: What parents and educators need to know about the emerging science of sex differences.* New York, NY: Random House.

Sax, L. (2009). *Boys adrift: Five factors driving the epidemic of unmotivated boys and underachieving young men.* New York, NY: Basic Books.

Sax, L. (2011). *Beyond pink and blue: What teachers need to know about the emerging science of sex differences.* Retrieved from Stetson University: http://www.stetson.edu/artsci/education/hollis-institute/media/seminar%20outline.pdf

Schiefele, U., & Csikszentmihalyi, M. (1995). Motivation and ability as factors in mathematics experience and achievement *Journal for Research in Mathematics Education, 26*(2), 163–181.

Schilling, D. L. (2006). Alternative seating devices for children with ADHD: Effects on classroom behavior. *Pediatric Physical Therapy, 18*(1), 81.

Schott Foundation. (2006). *Given half a chance: The Schott 50-state report on public education and black males.* Cambridge, MA: The Schott Foundation for Public Education.

Schwabe L., & Wolf, O. T. (2009). The context counts: Congruent learning and testing environments prevent memory retrieval impairment following stress. *Cognitive, Affective, & Behavioral Neuroscience, 9*(3), 229–236.

Sciutto, M., Nolfi, C., & Bluhm, C. (2004). Effects of child gender and symptom type on referrals for ADHD by elementary school teachers. *Journal of Emotional and Behavioral Disorders, 12*(4), 247–253.

Search Institute. (n.d.). *150 ways to show you care.* Retrieved from Search Institute: https://www.searchinstitutestore.org/150_Ways_p/0355-w.htm

Shindler, J. (2009). *Transformative classroom management: Positive strategies to engage all students and promote a psychology of success.* San Francisco, CA: Jossey-Bass.

Singh, D. (2002). *Emotional intelligence at work: A professional guide.* New Delhi, India: Sage.

Slocumb, P. (2004). *Hear our cry: Boys in crisis.* Highlands, TX: aha! Process.

Smith, M., & Wilhelm, J. (2002). *Reading don't fix no Chevys: Literacy in the lives of young men.* Portsmouth, NH: Boynton/Cook.

Smith, M., & Wilhelm, J. (2006). *Going with the flow: How to engage boys (and girls) in their literacy learning.* Portsmouth, NH: Boynton/Cook.

Stalvey, S., & Brasell, H. (2006). Using stress balls to focus the attention of sixth-grade learners. *Journal of At-Risk Issues, 12*(2), 7–16.

Steiner, C. (2003). *Emotional literacy: Intelligence with a heart.* Fawnskin, CA: Personhood Press.

Summerford, C. (2005). Action-packed classrooms: Movement strategies to invigorate K–5 learners. Thousand Oaks, CA: Corwin.

Sutarso, P. (1999). *Gender differences on the Emotional Intelligence Inventory (EQI).* Dissertation Abstracts International.

Thompson, M. (Director). (2006). *Raising Cain* [Motion picture]. Available for purchase at: http://www.pbs.org/opb/raisingcain/

Thompson, M., & Barker, T. (2008). *It's a boy: Understanding your son's development from birth to age 18.* New York, NY: Ballantine Books.

Tomlinson, B. (1998). Conclusions. In B. Tomlinson (Ed.), *Materials development in language teaching* (pp. 340–344). Cambridge, UK: Cambridge University Press.

Tyre, P. (2006, January 23). *The trouble with boys: A surprising report card on our boys, their problems at school, and what parents and educators must do.* New York, NY: Crown Publishers.

United States Bureau of Labor Statistics. (2011). *2011 Current Population Survey.* Retrieved from United States Bureau of Labor Statistics: http://www.bls.gov/cps/cpsaat11.pdf

Urban Studies Council. (2012, May). *A closer look at suspensions for African American males in OUSD.* Retrieved from AAMAI–A Partnership of the Urban Studies Council: http://www.urbanstrategies.org/aamai/

U.S. Department of Education. (2007). *America's high school graduates: Results from the 2005 NAEP high school transcript study.* Washington, DC: National Center for Education Statistics.

U.S. Department of Education. (2010). *Transforming American education: Learning powered by technology.* National Education Technology Plan. Retrieved from U.S. Department of Education: http://www.ed.gov/sites/default/files/netp2010.pdf

Walderhaug, E., Magnusson, A., Neumeister, A., Lappalainen, J., Lunde, H., Refsum, H., & Landro, N. (2007, September 15). Interactive effects of sex and 5-HTTLPR on mood and impulsivity during tryptophan depletion in healthy people. *Biological Psychiatry, 62*(6), 593–599.

Wanless, S. B., Patton, C. L., Rimm-Kaufman, S. E., & Deutsch, N. L. (2012). *Influences on implementation of the Responsive Classroom approach.* Retrieved from Responsive Classroom: http://www.responsiveclassroom.org/sites/default/files/pdf_files/Influences_Implementation_RC_Approach.pdf

Whitehouse, A., Mattes, E., Maybery, M., Sawyer, M., Jacoby, P., Keelan, J., & Hickey, M. (2012, July). Sex-specific associations between umbilical cord blood testosterone levels and language delay in early childhood. *Journal of Child Psychology and Psychiatry, 53*(7), 726–734.

Wolfe, P. (2011, September). *Brain research and education: Fad or foundation?* Retrieved from Mind Matters: http://patwolfe.com/2011/09/brain-research-and-education-fad-or-foundation/

Xu, X., Coats, J. K., Yang, C. F., Wang, A., Ahmed, O. M., Alvarado, M., . . . Shah, N. M. (2012). Modular genetic control of sexually dimorphic behaviors. *Cell, 148*(3), 596–607.

Zeff, T. (2010). *The strong, sensitive boy.* San Ramon, CA: Prana Publishing.

Index

CORWIN

A SAGE Company

The Corwin logo—a raven striding across an open book—represents the union of courage and learning. Corwin is committed to improving education for all learners by publishing books and other professional development resources for those serving the field of PreK–12 education. By providing practical, hands-on materials, Corwin continues to carry out the promise of its motto: **"Helping Educators Do Their Work Better."**